The All-American Justice System Handbook:

Handcuffs, Shower-shoes, and Visits

For Cross, Flip, Driz, Psyche, Rocky, Rahmel Lundy, Frye, Webb, & S. Haynes

Because if we would have knew,

We would not have had to do,

The lengths of time that we did.

Preface

Hollywood has created a false image of hell. It has stripped it of its cruelty, given it glamour, has mad it laughable, and in every sense sort of bearable. Because of this I would not use the word hell to describe my time in prison. That would discredit the daily horrors that were endured. From simple matters such as taking a shower with others who may want to test sample your "display", to things as serious as being in a facility with firing ranges up the road, knowing full well that the training going on is for aggression towards my children—the children of the lower-class.

For anyone who slips into the grips of this machine it will certainly be one of the most horrifying times of your life. The total vulnerability, the loneliness, and persistently harsh treatment is usually enough to damage the most durable of people. No one should ever want to come here, go there, or dangle anywhere in between. It is a slow death but not a certain death, and if you are able to survive, yours is a character society would need to appreciate.

It is very easy for others to say that you should never allow anyone or any situation take away from who you are. Never bearing witness to the hateful essence of one who dehumanizes at full blast they will only be able to assume that if it were them on the receiving end, they would do just as good. Their slick mouths sarcastically wishing us well. How we still smile, hold any type of giggle after this amazes me. I do know that most of us cannot cry because our tears were stolen from us living under years of truth.

Seeing that we are the accused from the time of our birth and that an arrest of one of us is an affirmation of their daily desires, are we innocent in this? Can we blame society or the white man or a dysfunctional system for our misstep? I say no, at a time when we were ignorant to the traps maybe but now, emphatically no.

Today is when we must take responsibility for us. In this well oiled machine that is running so smooth we must become the "sugar in the tank". The captive plays a major role in their captivity, without the cooperation of one the other cannot exist. Being angry at the captor for laying the trap while you watch as it is placed down and still run into it is misplaced anger. We are soldiers of the lower-class, the only ones who have courage enough to stand against the wrong and as soldiers we must behave as such…Hip-Hoppin' with compassion, love of self and serious discipline. We could be aware and progressive, spiritually enlightened and productive but without a structured determination from women and men battle tested in the halls of our open wounds we will continue to come up one point short.

I want no one to think that I am giving the reader everything that they will need, some lessons you will have to walk through on your own. Many of my peers will surely be the critics pointing out a slip or two. What do I say to them? Whatever I may have missed is for you to write a piece about, encouraging a healthy dialogue. See how this works? Your love for me, my love for you, our love for truth and struggle re-creates our world.

Min. Karim Jamal Johnson

THE BEGINNING

ARREST

You just got "knocked". Busted, pinched, bagged...caught. The jig is up kid, and you never saw it coming. As the handcuffs get tighter you start to think about how you should have listened to your girl when she asked you to stay home, or how it was her who ran you out. Maybe you're thinking about your mother telling you to watch who you are hanging around and asking you to be safe. One thing that is sure, there are fifty emotions running through your body. Anger, sadness, a few may even feel relieved, but most of all...stupid. You feel real stupid, and you should. But it's okay, we all have been there, even Jesus felt stupid when he was locked up. He just didn't have to eat the foul-ass cheese sandwiches that you are about to become very familiar with...the ones that are going to lock your bowels up as tight as too small Puma sneakers.

Yes feel stupid but not for too long because very soon you are going to have to use all of your smarts. Stop wondering if your partner got away or if the police found that gun that you tossed. Forget about the rest of the drugs in the stash or the chickenhead who you went to school with that saw you run by fast as the 'Flash' on speed. What you need to do right now is to keep in mind one thing...SHUT THE HELL UP! Do not say a word. From this point on keep your mouth closed. You do understand what I'm saying right, right? Then SHUT THE HELL UP! Just sit your butt down in the back of that police car and be quiet. Learn this from now and half the battle will be a breeze. What are we learning? That even a fish would not get into a fix if it kept its mouth shut.

PRECINCT

From this point on know that—POLICE DON'T LIKE YOU!—as you may have figured out already from the ride over. Some may laugh and joke about how long you're "going away for" or how easy it was to catch you. They get a good one in about that, especially if you were armed and did not bust a shot at them while you were fleeing. While they chuckle it up feel stupid again. Again it is okay because stupid or not we have all been there, so snap out of it, we still love you.

Your ride may not have been so sweet. You may have the luck of the Irish on your side and end up being arrested by sellout-ass Action Jackson and his sometimes lover Officer Peaches O' Neely, who both want to test out their new metal toys on your skull. I always remember one particular encounter when riding to the precinct during one of my many arrest, the driving officer so smoothly turned around to give me a gracious amount of his saliva for my face. I must have looked ashy after our tussle and jog covering about ten midtown blocks. After his gesture he politely informed me of how he'd "kill your black ass dead" after noticing my feet rose to show him my appreciation for his lovely gift. Either way your ride may go know that—POLICE DON"T LIKE YOU!—and you should –KEEP YOUR MOUTH SHUT. Don't tell them your name, don't say anything. If they're going to kill you, so be it, die with YOUR MOUTH SHUT. See the thing is that no matter how you were caught, how guilty you know that you are, the police don't have it all and are going to mess that arrest up. Unless of course you have been picked up by the feds, in which case you are finished. Never the less the same rules apply, for the simple fact that, the more that you open your mouth the more that the police will know. To cops anything that is said comes off as (and will be recorded as) a statement of guilt. You are not going to talk your way out of the arrest, remember—POLICE DON'T LIKE YOU—so KEEP YOUR MOUTH SHUT.

After the interrogation, what is known as the questioning and hot lamp treatment (that you see so often on television) you will be placed in a holding cell? A small, foul smelling place, sort of smells like old hot piss and musk. Get used to it; you will be in many more of these on this trip. Welcome to your first feel of bullpen therapy (sit back and get yourself together, I'll get back to bullpens later). The first thing that you will notice is that there is somebody in there with you. They may have been in there for the longest time you assume because of their appearance or maybe the police brought them in there a short time after you, either way do not speak to this person. 99% of the time this is a cop's informer. They were sent in there to get as much information as they can get. Never matter how insignificant you may think it is conversation in this situation is costly. Now most of these people are neighborhood people who owe "favors" to the police for various reasons and are always on call. You have never laid eyes on this person before in your life, and this is because 90% of the time people don't get arrested in the area that they live in. If you do happen to get arrested around your area you would never suspect that this person, whom you may have seen in passing or in fact dealt with at one time is a snitch. These are some dangerous people who must be corrected, but I'll get back to that later also.

This person is the crackhead who you may see fifty times a day, that dude drinking beer and smoking weed in front of the store all night, that nosey lady who never leaves the front of the housing complex. Do you remember that one day that you don't recall seeing them? No, they were not somewhere having sex with some other loser; they were in a precinct somewhere playing spy-games. Watch closely. No sooner than they will bum a smoke from you they will start a problem with the officers and catch the fake beatdown or they will start with a bundle of jokes get you laughing. I'm telling you right now who that is, so no matter what anybody else tells you or what you may tell yourself, resist all contact with this person. After a few hours of silence the police will move them out of that cell to another one and on to someone who has not read this book. The arresting officers will be angry because they have to fill out reports on what they know which at this point is nothing. If you listen you will have an edge going into the next round, and I can kiss myself for doing a good job so far. One more very important issue needs to be mentioned…the police can not make it easy for you with the D.A., which is the garbage that movies are filled with. Federal Agents are the only ones who can work magic making felonies vanish, however you will be in debt for life to them and that is not worth it.

THE SYSTEM & CENTRAL BOOKING

Things are about to get fun now. You are about to go through Central Booking the first stage of the System. If they have not found out who you are by now you have done an excellent job, but that ends here. You may have skirted around having your finger prints taken at the precinct but here they usually beat you up until they get your prints from you. The procedures may have changed over the years but not by much. In order for the system to work it must be regimental as well as repetitious, remember these are not the smartest people in the world.

You will be finger printed then strip searched. Yes, clothes off, everything. So now you see why you should never allow your girl to convince you to buy and wear that tight patent leather, light-blue and peach bikini briefs. Only a gay person keep some flashy stuff like that on their butt, and only gay people are really attracted to them as you are about to find out. If you have never experienced a one on one encounter with a gay person get ready for the beginning of what will be many such encounters. From this day forth you will live through about 5,000 of these dehumanizing acts. Right there in that stinky, filthy, gloomy cell you are about to be visually raped. It is what it is. And it is a form of rape because of the fact that the person who is forcing you to do this is being sexually gratified the whole time. Ask yourself who else would hold a job having to strip search a person of the same sex? They would either be a gay person or someone who is bisexual right? Right, there's no difference. This person will not only have to smell the cell but your funky body which has not showered for at the least past 48hrs. Seeing you in all your raw nakedness are not enough though, this person will also order you to spread your grippers. Yes your buttocks, your rear cheeks. Yeah that's right, turn around bend over and spread them. Now you feel cheap, this nasty bastard got a thrill and you are off to the next station.

If you haven't received a phone call by now for one reason or another you should get it around...now. Make it count! You know what you were picked up for and you know your felony status, if you feel that bail may be out of the question here is your opportunity to get your alibi straight (you'll see the importance of this in a few pages). Calm down whoever the person is that you called, and tell them to get whatever else is wrong corrected before any further police action comes about. The last thing that you're going to need is another felony, or worse, you being the cause of one of your people being charged with one. Let them know where you are at, what you were arrested for and if you are in good health or not. That is it! Do not go into any details for any reason over those phones. You should be directed to the next station soon but as you have figured out by now every minute that passes feels like an hour in here. At this stop you will be asked if you are hurt and in need of medical assistance, your vital signs will be taken and you will be asked if you are on or ever have been on drugs. Say no. Believe you me, say no! I don't care if you are the best crack smoker on the planet say no. Later on this small tip will save you from a lot of unnecessary drama.

This person may also write your bail report. Give the proper information here because this report will be used to determine if you will get an affordable bail. Make sure that the phone number that you give is the right number. Also make certain that the person who you gave as the contact is someone who knows your aliases that you are known by, as well as being someone who you know will be close to that phone. For some strange reason this is the only part of the system that works.

Within the next 12hrs you will be on your way to see a judge for arraignment. While you are waiting for this next step you will meet the courts appointed lawyer—the legal aid. You should know that by now rich people would have already had a discussion with their lawyer, more than likely three steps back at the precinct. Notice that I have said rich people, not white people. Justice is colorblind with the exception of the color green, always keep this in mind. You have not spoken to anyone so far so why start now, do you hear me? Excuse this person, don't say anything. More than likely this person is a snake, if you stare at them long enough they will get mad and go away. Do not worry about upsetting this person; believe me you may run through 3 or 4 of these legal aids before one of them shows you that they just might work for you and not the courts. It is going to take everything inside of you to keep your mouth closed at this point especially when you hear the way this person speaks down to you and showing that you are guilty until proven innocent. Get angry because believe what I'm telling you, you have every right to be, but just hold out for a few minutes more.

You are now called to appear before the judge…now speak. Speak loud, damn it yell if you want to; just make it clear that you would like to testify before the grand jury. This legal aid snake is going to ask you to be quiet and to speak directly to her or him; the judge may say something as well but damn them both. Damn them! Say it again nice and loud "I want to testify before the grand jury" and say it two more times. Everyone is going to be mad at you, the judge is going to order you to be quiet but say it to him too. It is important that you get this on record and this is what you are doing. Anything that is said in open court is recorded and you want to have your request for grand jury appearance on record. The grand jury is your one shot at beating this thing before it gets deeper. By upsetting the judge you may have just blown your chance at a reasonable bail but so what, if you can convince the grand jury of your innocence you are out of this mess right then and there.

If it has been anywhere between 24-72hrs since your arrest kid you doing well. However this also tells me that you are a newjack or a veteran who waited too long in their criminal career to play this game. There was a time when it took seven days before you appeared in front of a judge. Yes seven whole days, six of them moving from precinct to precinct, from stink cell to stink cell and from informer to informer. Seven days of watching the foulest of the homeless while they pick their noses and scratch themselves, and move their bowels in plain view. Of course we can not forget the bonus prize…seven days of knuckle to knuckle action, mainly for trying to avoid becoming a robbery victim. Someone probably figured out that 24hrs was enough time to keep the weak from ending up having to come out from the holding cells, and appear in front of the judge with one shoe on, torn trousers and a very nice black-eye.

After seeing the judge (and if you've done your job), enraging the whole courtroom and stating that you want to testify before the grand jury your bail will be set. Here is where the rich go and hug their very supportive families while the poor people get to find out the true meaning of the terms "public restroom", "traveling with everything you own on your back", and "only the strong survive". Here is where the poor people get to taste the county jail.

COUNTY JAIL

For most of the country the previous pages were foreign to you. This is how it has gone down in NYC, another way in which we are unique though the prison process worldwide is pretty much the same at this next step…the dreadful county jail, Rikers Island for us. On your ride to your new home away from home forget about the stress for a minute, this is the time to get focused. You are about to enter a world where basically no one gives a damn about you! Do you dig me, especially if you are one of those "off the block dudes" as we call them? You know the type that doesn't get around much, commits neighborhood felonies, and only family members or ex-classmates think that you are dangerous. Yes you. No one in there could care less how mad you get or how tough you think you may be, so listen close if you want to keep all of your fingers and toes.

BE on POINT

Everyone should be familiar with the term "be on point" yet it still surprises me that so few people actually practice what comes out of their mouths. No one is going to take care of you like you will, now more than ever you must be serious in this task. Notice your surroundings keeping your ears and eyes open with your back to the wall. No one knows who you are, most probably wouldn't like you and love is a far reach up. There is only filth, hate and hunger in these walls so get used to dealing with it and staying mentally awake. None of us are nice people and if in this situation we can make your life worse we will. If something can be taken from you it will be took, the taking of your shoes, the taking of your joy, or the taking of your life.

BULLPEN THERAPY

The past few days have been pure hell. You are stressed to the limit, hungry and most of all tired. You have not slept, how could you? With roaches dancing around and the occasional crackhead or two begging you for cigarettes that you don't have, sleeping even for a second is close to impossible. Not to mention that you can not keep from watching that teenager over in the corner who has kept his one good eye on your wrist watch. Right now you would do just about anything to get out of here; this is what being confined does to a person. It is constant aggravation with subtle pressure that we call bullpen therapy. Make an attempt to remain strong and not allow this to break you. As you will come to find out there will be many hours spent in bullpens during your stay in the system. For you to keep your mental intact and somewhat calm during these sit-ins is an unquestioned necessity.

What I usually do is immediately make a scan of the whole pen before I step in so I can find a clear spot. Make a quick count of how many people are in there and try to feel what's going on. The tension in the air is always present don't worry about it, if you can sit-down somewhere sit, and there is standing room only most of the time which is not a bad thing. Listen to all conversations, pay attention to all movements no matter how subtle. Observing how strange people become once they have to deal with their inner-self is very calming. Stay out of those very loud debates especially if you were not invited to give your opinion. If by chance you are invited to join in politely decline but do not come off as being distant, which will arouse suspicion and could get you beat up.

Upon entering the bullpen at the county jail you will see all types of people doing all types of things, all at various stages of their lock-up. Some are leaving out of the jail to go to court, while others are returning from court. A few are either going or coming back from outside medical trips. Then there is you and the bunch of people that came in at the same time that you did. Out of all the people in the pen you all will be the last ones to leave that pen. Not only because correction officers are slow (real slow) but because you have to be processed into the system.

INTAKE

As you should already know everyone in jail has a number, and now so will you. All the important information will be given by you here. You know, your emergency contact, religion, gang affiliation (a new one for us in NYC but very common elsewhere) and known enemies. More finger prints are taken, as well as more photos. You may be stunned by how pretty the officer handling all of this is but snap out of it, you will rarely if ever see this officer again. Though you shouldn't worry there are many more in the back. Based on the information you provided security will classify you in terms of risk factor. Either you are high, medium or low classification, PC (Protective Custody) or Administrative Segregation. Once you are classified you will be placed in the next available housing unit.

HOUSING UNIT

Lesson 1:

Fix your face. I explained to you a little while ago that no one gives a damn about you. Contrary to popular belief tough looking faces and slick tough talk does not make you a tough person. The real tough people see right through that. Even if you are tough you are new to this particular place and the numbers are against you so be easy.

Again scan your surroundings and feel the area out. You are on point and your mouth is shut. Do know however, that half of your story is already told. Everyone knows that you are new to the system. How you ask? Because you walked in with no property silly…not to mention you look a mess and pee-yew…you smell!! Not that you can do anything about it yet (you still have no cosmetics), even if you could there is no way that you are comfortable enough to get in the shower without knowing who is who in the unit.

Lesson 2:

Someone is in control. Your job is to find out whom. It is much easier to find out who is in charge if it is a dormitory as oppose to a celled housing unit. Whatever type of unit it is you are still going to have to wait until everybody is in there. So while you wait until the unit is at full capacity you need to clean up where you are supposed to lay your head and check out the rest of the area.

Lesson 3:

Don't touch the phone. Depending on what time of day it is you may interfere with someone's "slot time". The phone and television are tools of power in the county jail. Yes I know this is very silly but it is just that. Until you know for sure how things are running wait a while before you make an attempt to reach out and touch someone, someone may be waiting in the wings to touch you. I'll come right back to the phones and television in a second.

Lesson 4:

You don't know that "homie" from around your way like you think you do. You have checked everything out, cleaned your area up nicely, and then all of a sudden, "Yo Family, what's up!" Someone from your neighborhood calls out to you. Of course the natural reaction is to feel good while approaching to greet them; you may even feel a bit relieved. A familiar face is always a plus in an unfamiliar environment...or so it is perceived. Understand me here. This person may be more relieved to see you than you could ever be to see them so hold off on some of that excitement while you do a little investigating.

When moving from street to prison, housing unit to housing unit, from county jail to a state facility or from prison to prison there are always going to be people that you will run into who you would consider as someone that you "know" pretty well. They say that separation may make the heart grow fonder but it also gives time for bullshit to get into the mix of one's life. Now you may have grown up around this person, they could be a classmate or even a past crime-partner who you may have committed felonies with, but unless you have spent 24hrs a day everyday with them you could be in for a lumpy trip opening up your doors to them, give it two days; quite enough time for a persons' true character to emerge. You may not have seen this person for six weeks, maybe six months or even six years all of which are eternities in jail.

Please hold on to this...you no longer "know" this person you know of them. There is nowhere else on the face of this planet where the term "you are judged by the company that you keep" taken as total truth as it is in here. Your "homie" may be a snitch, might have been engaging in homosexual activity, and could be in debt to a jailhouse drug dealer or have a major beef that you won't know about until your blood is spilling out all over the dayroom floor and that's not a good way to start off your stay here.

Everybody knows a little info about everything on everyone behind these walls so get a run down on your "homie" from a believable source. Witness how people move when "homie" is around and how they speak to him. Find out how others feel about him, but of course be subtle and crafty, you don't want to alert your "homie" to your suspicions because the situation could become very nasty.

HEALTH AND HYGEINE

Okay the investigation is going down and you are not playing your "homie" too close but you're no fool either. You are going to need a few things until your people on the outside can get to you, important things. No not cigarettes foolio. Cosmetics, you know soap and toothpaste and other items such as washcloths that this person may have. So be cool and get whatever you need from them because now it is time to scrub that funky butt.

SHOWERS

As you will soon see the bullpens are not the only area that is filthy in jail. Just about the whole place could be considered a toxic landfill. From where you rest your head to where you eat, to where you wash—this place is flooded with germs, fungus and bacteria. The showers are the number one spot for this though. There are no less than fifty people using maybe 3 or 4 shower slots at any given time daily. That is many more than the 4 or 5 people that shared the shower in your home, and might I add that these are not the cleanest people in the world. County jails hold homeless people, drug addicts, mentally ill people and young people (who for some reason think that being dirty is cool).

It doesn't matter what kind of cleaning supplies the administration may give you to clean up with, and no matter how many times you clean up the place is still going to be foul. Most county jails are old, very old, so the grime and filth just sets in. To add to it already being filthy you have so many people doing so many disgusting things in the shower (such as masturbating, urinating and spitting) that it will never be sanitary.

First things first, before you go in the shower area as always stay on point. Look and see who is in the shower area before you get prepared to go in. Catching an empty shower area is rare but it happens more than one would think. Get everything that you need from the cell or locker and get busy. Have in mind that you are going to get in and get out, no playing around. This is the county jail and anything that can go down will. Believe me, you do not want to be one of the few who happen to be in the shower when the CO's bust in to do a unit search, it is the most humiliating feeling. Though you will see others playing "grab-ass" and chit-chatting in the shower this won't be you. Why, because you are reading this wonderful book. I do have to mention that there is a person who no matter what time of day it is always happen to be in the area (we'll get back to this clown upstate).

Try not to touch anything with your bare skin. No leaning on the walls or touching the faucets more than you need to. It seems to take no time for a rash or something worse to get up on you. My only time being infected with crabs was at Rikers Island. I don't know if they came from the showers or the mattress, but I do know that I saw a dude plucking stuff off his skin and scratching and slapping at himself in the bathroom. This guy ended up infecting the whole unit of 30 men. That was about 15yrs ago and I've been bald down there ever since. Of course I get strange looks during strip searches or when a dude may glance over in the shower, but I could care less I'm clean and bug free. This brings me to my next point.

As I said earlier if you catch an empty shower you are fortunate. Other than that this will be a group setting so all hang-ups about nudity should be checked at the door. We are all the same sex and want the same thing…the opposite sex. You may question the people who seem to be in the shower for what appears to be all day, especially that clown who has been there since like yesterday. Most of us have participated on sports teams, served in the military or are just comfortable with ourselves enough not to freak out in this situation. My "presentation" is proper, not the biggest and not the smallest. Dudes are not going to chuckle at my "joint" and most of the women that I've shared him with found him to be "rather handsome". Until that is, they got up on him and tried to…anyway. Where was I? Oh yeah...clean your body and get out of there, you are trying to wash and not catch anything.

IN THE AIR

Having so many people in such a small space is very unhealthy especially without the proper ventilation, just look up. Do you see all that thick dust around the bars, windows and vents? Look as if it has not been cleaned in year's right? That's because it hasn't. It is very important that you are aware of this. In order to leave this place the way that you came in (healthy) keep in mind that only you care about what happens to you. There are people with HIV, hepatitis (all strains), tuberculosis and AIDS all around you. If you are not part of the cleaning crew (house gang, porters) within your first few days there get on it quick. This gives you access to as much of the cleaning supplies that are available. Do you remember how they treated you in the clinic coming through intake, not the best healthcare providers of the bunch are they?

CLINIC

What do you mean you don't remember passing through here? It's probably because you were half sleep by the time they called your name. We understand, but let's see if we can jar your memory. Do you remember it becoming real cold all of a sudden, the lights beaming bright and having to step over that dope-fiend who smelled like urine and vomit? You remember that right? Good. So I don't have to remind you how rude the staff was and how they handled you. As Stevie Wonder once sang, I have "these three words" for you. DON"T GET SICK! These are not the most talented group, the whole of them graduated at the bottom percentage of their class if at all.

A trip to "sick call" is at least 3hrs and starts at six in the morning. Only the worse of the worst take that trip to the clinic or the most extreme of emergencies. Never let these people in here experiment with you, if they do not know what is wrong with you from your symptoms do not let them try to figure it out. These are people who love to prescribe generic medications, do not be a lab-rat. If you feel for any reason that the nurse or doctor you are in front of is not proper get up and leave. That is your body, you only have one why let some prison quack ruin it for the rest of your life.

PHONES

You've gotten out of the shower and you feel human again but you still have on the same foul clothes that you were arrested in. You may have even borrowed an outfit from your "homie" but this is so not you. You usually don't get down like that and you want your own stuff, it is time to get on that phone.

All housing units have some sort of power structure. Whether it is the quietest unit in the jail or the most dangerous unit, someone or some group is in charge and running things. As people move in and out of the unit power shifts accordingly. This power is established by the act of taking control and manipulating the usage of one or all of three of the following items: the phone, the television, and the food wagon. One person may have all the power (rarely), a few people split the power (usually) or a gang has the power. Unquestionably the phone is the most important symbol of power being that it is the main source to the outside world.

The standard schedule for the phone is set up based around how the administration feels we should use it. Of course we have other ideas about that. The phones are electronically turned on at 8am and shut off at 10:45pm. Most off the housing units are run in this manner. For general population (people who are not connected to any power set) and new people coming into the unit the phone time is from 8am-6pm, everybody else holds a "slot time" running from 6pm until the phones shutoff. A "slot" is a position in line or a place on the phone schedule that people have taken by force through fighting, cutting, stabbing. There are times when a "slot" or whole phone schedule is inherited, this causes major problems. When you have "slot time" in a housing unit you usually have some type of authority in the unit. Some people wait for months for a "slot"; others get them as soon as they walk through the door. The bottom line is that there will be trouble if whoever is using that phone is not on at the proper time.

During your stay in the county you will see people who you may think don't deserve their "slot time". You may hear them screaming at their people through the phone to "come up and see me" or sweet-talking about something trivial while you are attempting to get in touch with your lawyer. You want to take care of business and they're playing "phone-games". This could be true but no one can say whose situation is more important, theirs or yours. To avoid conflict just ride it out until you get your own "slot" which is usually a 30 minute time span.

The phones were operated at a free of charge rate for years until the administration felt that they could tone down the violence by controlling the factors that determine the usage. They once worked the same as the phones in your home where all you have to do was pick up and dial a number for a call of unlimited time, with call waiting and all. This was replaced with a computer system that has a setting on it which limits calls based on your identification number. You are now charged .33 per call which is now broken down into 6 minutes per call and only 21mins per ID number, however you are allowed to use your ID number once every 5hrs. If you think that the level of violence never changed you are right. The truth of the matter for the system change, and administrative control of the phone is that, the less access that you have to the outside world the harder it will be to properly defend yourself in court.

TELEVISION & DAYROOM

Your conversation was stressful and if anything else a disheartening wake-up call for you and your peoples. You gave them a list of what you need, the schedule for visits and your exact location (housing unit). There is nothing else that you can do right now so just fall back and relax.

In county jail we can do a lot of one of two things, a whole lot of reading (progressive) or a whole lot of bullshitting (regressive). Most of the bullshitting is done in the television area or dayroom. Usually this is a small area with a few tables and chairs in front of an aged vision impaired, muffled sound giving box of a television. Of course you know that this is always a red-zone. The number of people who have been knocked-out, sliced or stabbed because of the television is so high that they should re-name it the "battle box". After witnessing and at times participating in a good number of these brawl-for-it all type of affairs I discovered a couple of methods of safety.

1. Know the area: Before you go in the dayroom look at the size of the area. See if there is more than one way out and how much space is available per person. Notice how many people are in there regularly and at what times.

2. Know what's going on inside: Are people getting high inside? Do they stash weapons in there? Are there other activities going on (i.e. card playing, chess, dominos) that would make it difficult for you to relax.

3. Keep your back to the wall: Never sit or stand with your neck out, especially when your attention is being diverted.

4. Their debate is their debate: Stay in your own conversation, you may be absolutely correct…however no one asked you.

Remember we were not the ones voted "most likely to succeed" we were the class knuckleheads, always in trouble and being thrown out of the class...not a very polite bunch at all and some not too bright. That's how we found our way here. So just because you may feel a 44yr old person has no business watching Tiny-Toons that should not be a reason for you to hurt somebody or have somebody hurt you. They may feel that the news is not all that special. In other words we all have opinions on what's important, in order to live as comfortable as possible in here we must respect the next person's space.

Take for an example this very true incident of one dude who either chose to ignore the rules or just plain forgot where he was.

One evening after another very aggravating housing unit search the always probable and most times inevitable popped-off. Minutes after getting the unit back in order two dudes decided to dance. Well one wanted to dance the other was I believe just making a lot of noise. A young Latino brother no more than 20yrs old and tiny, only about 5'3" and 125lbs, new to the unit but very observant was quietly watching television. Out of nowhere come the 'Dred', 6'2" and 240lbs who have been in the housing unit 8 months and way too comfortable with his "position" gives the young fellow a crazy look while turning the channel. Of course the young fellow is perplexed and it shows as he looks around yet says nothing. 'Dred' starts to rant and rave about how he's the "biggest motherfucker in here and going to start knocking these new dudes out for touching things in here!" then sits down to watch "his show". I'm only guessing here but I think the young fellow took that as a request to tango because as 'Dred' leaned back in his favorite chair after a commercial break…the young fellow enthusiastically made an incision from one side of 'Dred's' neck to the other.

Amusingly 'Dred' sprinted towards the front gate to alert the authorities about his condition which was obvious. I mean his blood was everywhere but the young fellow was not finished. He went over to 'Dred' as he was yelling for the correction officers and stabbed him in the back. Then he called for the authorities himself and walked back to the cell that he was staying in to lay down.

You see unknown to all of us, especially 'Dred', the young fellow was back down from upstate to go to court. He was already serving 25yrs to life for a murder conviction and was back in the county preparing for trial on two more murders. As expected the squad came to take the young fellow to the box so we never did get to find out if he was ever convicted of those other two homicides, but we do know from the investigation of the city police and our two week lockdown that the 'Dred' died from his injuries.

So be easy, this is not home and you are not alone. If you do not like or aren't interested in what is being watched on the television, or can't hear it because of the noise in the dayroom just get up and go to your spot so you can read a book. Take it from me it will be time much better spent.

VISITS and PACKAGES

Many counties of the country, at the county jail level still have booth visits and I do feel for you. Booth visits are no touch visits like the ones you see on television and in the movies, with the glass partition and plastic phone, a very savage encounter. However in NYC, our visits are full contact unless for some disciplinary reason that privilege is taken from you. Other than that we get to do our thing.

Visits on Rikers Island are at a minimum one hour in duration, and depending on who you are or how you carry yourself—a maximum two and a half to three hours. Whatever amount of time you get I suggest that you make it count. There is a lot of important business that needs to be discussed and every second is precious. Don't waste time arguing or giving your people the angry silent treatment because they were not able to do something that you felt was top priority. Remember they are stressed out too, not as stressed as you and could never feel that totally but they are stressed to a degree. Their reaction time to move accordingly in this situation is a hell of a lot slower than ours, so be patient and don't act up. With everything that they had to go through to get to visit you the last thing you want to do is add on to their unpleasant experience or seem unappreciative.

From the point of them having to build up enough courage within themselves to come visit you, to the ride and having to deal with the foul mouthed other visitors, and the nasty attitude correction officers…the trip is not something that they look forward to regardless of how much they miss you. They resent coming and resent the fact that you are here. They resent having to go through the body search, the long lines for dropping off packages and putting money in your account. Truthfully they don't want to come here about as much or more than you not wanting to be here, but if you act as their gracious guide you have the ability to make this journey smooth and refreshing.

First thank your people for coming. I don't care if it's your mother, husband or cousin. No one is obligated to go on this trip with you. Don't just show them that you are appreciative by smiling like a clown all visit, tell them with words because it adds to the sincerity.

Next apologize to them for any ill treatment that they may have received on the way in. Again this is to let them know that even at the worse stage of your life you are concerned about their well being. Ask them to also excuse the behavior of the others on the visiting floor. The fighting, the over-hyper children, and the sex-acts are not true representations of those involved. Held in unnatural conditions we all have the potential to be other than ourselves. Huh, it can only be expected that once days turn into months of being away from your significant other that you too are going to yearn for an impromptu "touch & sniff" session. Make note though, in order to keep who you are with with you, keep these sessions few in number. To tease a lover and send them out into the world of easy access is not too smart of a move.

Packages should be kept simple, get what you need to live. Many county jails do not allow their populations to receive packages forcing you to survive solely on what the institution provides for you, another burden that we happen to escape here in NYC. We are not allowed to have food sent in but cosmetics, reading materials and clothes are all allowed. You will see everything from Versace' to Sean John and from gator-skin shoes to ADIDAS in here. My advice to you is to again keep it simple. There are no washing machines, no irons and no way to properly maintain that $400.00 crushed silk number you got at the spring clearance. At the county jail you will be moved from housing unit to housing unit for various reasons so losing clothes is a given. This is a perfect time to ease out of the materialism that helped land you here in the first place. Get items that are easy to wash since you'll be washing by hand, and that dry relatively quickly. Sweat-suits are excellent; they are all purpose and even when inexpensive can look presentable. These are also clothes that you won't be too offended when they get thrown around during a cell search.

THE SEARCH

There are several types of searches all of which will anger you some more so than others. There are facility searches, housing unit searches, cell searches and body searches. Then you have the unnecessarily annoying searches like the "going to the yard", "going to the law library", "coming from a visit", and the "Hey! What are you doing over here?! Get on the wall!"…search. A few of these calls for you to strip down to your nakedness, most of them allow the authorities to put their nasty hands on you and rifle through your stuff. The reason given for this constant harassment is the need to maintain "security", however this is a tactic that is believed to break your fighting spirit through daily humiliation. Now you never have to participate with the program, you can always refuse a search, just keep in mind that refusal of a search is an express ticket to the box.

Nothing is more upsetting than a random cell search. You will know that it's coming yet and still the frequency of the nonsense is difficult to swallow and ignore. One way to create a buffer between you and the agitation is to not have a lot of personal items. Keep as few things as possible in that cell. This is not home and no matter what you may have you will never become comfortable here. Keep pictures, magazines and books to a minimum because the authorities love to throw those around. I've witnessed them knock Korans and Bibles in the toilet as well as stomp on unopened packs of cookies, chips and other snacks. Yes it is real foul, but its okay, you'll be back on the street soon and then it will be your turn to "search" someone.

There are a couple of ways to work around this. One way is to live in a mess so disastrous that it would be no fun for them to wreak havoc upon your tiny dwelling. But this way is not to safe, healthy or smart considering the fact that you will never know what is in that cell with you. Not to mention that in a mess anything could be planted in there by anyone, understand me? The other way to beat the drama of a search is to go totally opposite from the first way and live impeccably clean. Have nothing in visible sight and nothing that the authorities would consider special to you, this ensures a quick exit from your area the majority of the time. When all else fails wait until the officer that is searching you is arm close and let go some of the most lethal anal gas that you've got. You know the silent quick to reach the nose deadly stuff. I'll bet my last dollar that they will not only run up out of there but that they will remember you and not be so fast to run up in and disrespect your area. This works well for those spur of the moment spot frisks too.

COMMISSARY

Commissary is another privilege that I found to be nonexistent in many county jails. Again I do have empathy for those who have to survive on what their captors feed them. I'd invite you all to come do crime in NYC but we really are making an honest attempt at changing the criminal mentality to a progressive lifestyle. Those who have come here do know that you'll never find more hospitable turnkeys, tasty treats or legal loopholes.

If it were not for the commissary many of us would damn near starve to death in the county jail. The food items that can be purchased are by no means the most nutritious in fact they consist of sugar, sugar and more sugar. Candy bars, cookies, cupcakes, donuts, chips and kool-aid. They may also have a few items with a little more substance like instant oatmeal, soups, packaged cold-cuts and sandwich rolls. This is the stuff to stack up on being that commissary is only once a week and you're going to eat those sweets in three days. A trick that I learned is to buy a couple of items that I'm not to fond of, this way when all the flavor (favorite) snacks are gone I'll still have something to hold me over until the next time I am able to shop. Because different housing units shop on different days and there is always a possibility of you being moved you should always try to keep extra commissary, never be caught without because believe me only a few share, and you could end up in a housing unit that shops 5 days after you get there.

FOOD

I'm not going to waste too much space here. The garbage that they try to pass off as food is horrible. There is never any taste, all the wrong texture and way off temperature. Even after years of in and out of this situation it still baffles me, how do we survive? There's this one recipe of barbeque beef over rice that has to be the meal from hell. I bullshit you not, the rice is as hard as a pair of dice and the beef you would swear is nothing less than knuckles, kneecaps and elbows taken from the last few people who were dragged off to the hole(solitary confinement). The definition of non-edible begins and ends here.

LAW LIBRARY

Just think of this as a place of secrets, the answers of all questions that have to do with you getting back to your family, the ultimate think tank. It is a place where I suggest you get to whenever you have the opportunity. This is another area where it's best to be on point and keep your mouth shut. As with anywhere else in the building the law library is known for explosive behavior at the most serene times. As with the yard, visiting room area and bullpen, people from different housing units who wouldn't usually run across each other are side by side in this small space. Most of the time in here it is uneventful but it is never quiet which for a library is always distracting.

Even if you are not the most literate person in the world, that should not keep you from striving to acquire some knowledge of the law and how it applies to you and your case. No one, I repeat no one is an expert when it comes to this stuff though there are some people who are very sharp when it comes to working it. The more that you study the law yourself the better you will be at figuring out who is sharp with it and who is not. There is no quick method for testing this because of how everyone will sound as if they really know what the hell it is they are doing. Please know that it will be a long run of trial and error. When you do not know the correct way of finding the information that you need ask for help, ask for explanations, ask for honesty. Don't let people tell you what you want to hear, this is the place to be very real with yourself and the situation.

Okay here's where things get tricky, especially if you have never come through the system prior to this. You're going to have to tell someone the facts of your case. Someone like whom, one of those sharp people who you'll grow to trust. Now you're going to have others say to you that you should never tell anyone about your case for various reasons, main reason being that anything you say can and will be used against you. There are people who will find out information about a big enough case and try using it as a "get out of jail free" card. Use your wit and when you do find someone that you feel comfortable with do not lie to them. Don't leave out important information because it will not do anything but hamper your cause. Besides most people who have worked in here have heard thousands of cases and can tell when certain parts of a story don't sound right. Why would you or any smart person have someone who is trying to help them run around searching for laws or codes that may not pertain to your case? Only you know the particulars so only you can help you. Remember this person is one of us to some degree and not the court appointed sell-out that the DA is making deals with.

I have to tell you that it is not all good with some of us either. Remember where you are, those around you are some very grimy people too. Knowing the law and how to apply it is very profitable for anyone so most won't help you for the love of the art. In prison as well as on the outside legal work is a hustle and just like a mechanic of autos the jailhouse lawyer is going to fix just enough to keep you coming back for his services. Thus the importance again of learning as much as you can yourself. Before I move on I need to address one more issue. Forget that talk you hear..."If they are so good how come they can't get themselves out of jail, how come they're still locked up?" Forget this nonsense! This ignorance is as silly as asking a doctor why she can't keep herself from catching a cold. Some people were captured in a way that no matter what they do they're staying in jail. This by no means should be held as a scale on how much they can assist your non-understanding the law behind. Understand me?! At times information comes from the most unlikely sources; make sure that you pick some of it up.

Note: This section should be ignored if you were capture by the federal government. You can basically fall back and wait until they make you an offer that you can't refuse. If you are in the federal system you all should know by now that talking to anyone about your case is a definite no-no.

THE YARD

There are very few county jails that still use a gymnasium for their populations' recreational activities. Ask anyone from the administration the reason for this is and they'll be quick to tell you that it is much safer for the detainees in a visually open area or that recreational activity is healthier in an outdoor environment. The truth is that after many run-ins with swift footed people who have legitimate grievances and sharp metal objects in their hands they found that being in a closed gym wasn't too smart for the people in uniform.

The yard is the heart of every county jail, correctional facility, prison or penitentiary. The mood of the institution is based on the mood of the yard. If the yard is in a wild energy the housing units will be wild, if there's beef in the yard there will be beef in the unit. A session of recreation in the yard usually last for about an hour and if at the end of that hour everyone goes back inside smiling nine times out of ten it will be a good night. The administration knows this so this is one spot that they tend not to bother you. It does not mean that they are not watching every move out there.

Doing what we do and being the innovators that we are we turned the yard into a place, on many different levels, somewhere that substitutes for our outside communities. It has become our hood, set, town and ward; our streets, blocks, avenues and corners so unsurprisingly the same activities take place. Sports are played and drug deals are made. Gays are propositioning and rivals are positioning. Many are getting high but some are just out there to show that they can still get "Fly". In the midst of all this very strong bonds are being made. Whoever you walk the yard with is usually the person(s) that you trust with your life so know who you are walking with. This is serious business. As far as the other activities use your common sense. When it comes to playing sports I don't indulge. For one reason, I have no time or room for injury while being surrounded by officers of the state. Reason two is the fact that sports, card games, board games and such give others an open door that may be used to say things to you that they may have never been allowed to say, disrespectful things.

For those of us who work-out (exercise) I have only one suggestion and that is to find a partner or team that is reaching for goals similar to yours. If you're working-out just to past the time or to look good on the beach when you get out of jail, then a team who is training to prepare for war are the wrong people for you. I usually look for the crazy person, the dude who is sort of offbeat and is on brain medication or should be on it. The kind of person who I know that after the work-out I'm going to be cursing their mother for birthing them. This is what I need because it keeps me honest, never leaving any room for slacking off. A crazy person may be a lot of different people but they won't cheat themselves, and they for damn sure not going to let you cheat. Also as an added bonus there are not too many people who are going to try to attack a person who is known to be a little off mentally. Knowing that should give you a little extra sense of security while in the yard and we all could use that.

COP-OUT or TRIAL

This may be the most important decision of your life. To either plead guilty to the crime that you are charged of (cop-out) or go to trial. As I wrote previously no one knows the elements of your case but you, so no one can advise you to choose either way. I will tell you that the conviction rate for low-income people without proper representation in court is about eight out of ten in the favor of the prosecution. That's eight people out of every ten who take their cases to trial that will be on their way to an upstate prison for a very long time.

What is important for you to understand is that just because the district attorney puts an offer on the table that does not mean that she/he feels unsure about winning the case, no-no please throw to the side that kind of thinking. The reason for any kind of offer that allows you to "plead out" to a lesser charge is that at this point of the prosecutions' investigation, with the evidence that they have, they'll settle for that amount of offered time from you. The more evidence that they gather to better there case and the longer you take to decide whether or not to accept the offered time becomes a major factor in the number of years that your life will be on hold. This is not a department store, not an auction house. To haggle with these people and give them any extra time to seal your fate is not too smart. I'm not advising you to cop-out to something that you did not do, where you were not involved in the act or was nowhere around. No I'm not doing that. I am just telling you to know when to take yours.

I also urge you to be very mindful of the clowns around you who are in your ear saying "The DA ain't got nothing on you, you going home. I had a case just like that and got it thrown out. This is my fourth felony…don't cop-out to that bullshit." This is the person you stay away from because listening to this dumb-ass will have you in prison for life. Yes it may very well be their fourth felony, wonder why? How has this person managed to ride the wave of the system without a total wipe-out? Why has the beast's belly rejected this piece of prime meat?

The answer is simple…this clown always took a plea-deal, something that the clown is telling you not to do. There are many people that you will come across who have been to prison numerous times for all types of felonies, every one of them able to walk the street again because they were smart enough or advised not to go to trial. In all my years of riding the wave I have met very few and I stress very few people who have gone to trial more than once. Anyone who has any sense of life and death will tell you that going to trial is what the rest of the world would define as terrorism. It is a horrific experience that I for one will never go through again.

Note: There is another dumb statement, and it is "If you blow (loose) trial you can get an appeal." Well I blew trial and did get an appeal…5yrs later and 3yrs after that I'm still here writing this book.

Now never ever cop-out to a life sentence, I don't care if it is one year to life. When it comes to that you may as well take your chances with a jury. Just don't be a clown do your own math.

SENTENCING

You have lost your case, a jury of your peers has convicted you and today you have come to receive the punishment. Come to court today relaxed and relieved knowing that this is the end of the beginning. Your shoulders should feel a hell of a lot lighter and your brain much more focused for the journey ahead. The judge will give you an opportunity to say anything that you may want to say before she states how much time they expect for you to do. This is not the time and she is not the person to be in front of raving about injustice, standing all political as Rev. Al or Huey Newton, no. Remember you just blew trial or you took a plea thus admitting guilt so address the judge in a clear voice accepting responsibility for your role in the act; apologize to your family, the victims and the court. As a matter of fact it wouldn't hurt if you wrote what you were going to say the night before. No judge is going to take points off if you read instead of trying to memorize it. All this comes back into play when the time comes for you to appear before the parole board. Let no one tell you any different it will be looked at.

From this point on your grippers belong to the state so keep an eye on them. Have your family or whoever it is that is supporting you right now get your first package ready for the state system from now to avoid any delay. These items are a few of the basics that you will need:

Cosmetics

Tuna   Thermals (yes even if it's summer)

Snacks   canned fruit

Underwear   Sweat-suits

 Socks   Hooded sweat-shirt

                                  Books

Let's go upstate.

THE MIDDLE

Up north…here we come.

RECEPTION

If you have never been to the south by car or taken a ride outside of the city the first thing that you will notice about being transferred upstate is how spacious the world is. There are miles and miles of highway and open land, trees and grass, mountains and all of this a mere 40mins out from the city. You will also find out that at the end of back roads, along side small towns and tucked away neatly from any concerning vision are places filled with unimaginable human hate. Places with total disregard for life and energy so rotten that it corrupts the purest soul. Welcome to the Governor's house.

BULLPEN (Upstate)

As you have already heard on the bus ride up very clearly from the pleasantly unattractive officer, "This is not the county jail, this is not Rikers Island! Follow instructions or you will hurt yourself!" The funny thing is that I have never hurt myself, not intentionally at least but I found out fast what they meant because one move too slow or too fast and these officers will jump on you. Now the average age of these frail out of shape scruffy 'Farmer Joe' looking guys is anywhere from 40-48yrs old. You are a tough guy yourself and known in your neighborhood as the pound for pound best fighter. However after these guys jump you you'll swear that you was back in grade school on the ground being kicked and punched and stepped on by the Lawton family for pulling baby sister Tamika's ponytail while taking her .25 taffy. Not a nice feeling.

Do not take what I'm saying as a statement to put fear in your heart, no, you should never be fearful of these people, most of them want no trouble and the few who want problems are cowards, this is why they gang up on you. Again, my statement is to encourage you to be cautious and to emphasize the fact that POLICE DON'T LIKE YOU!

Here in reception is where you have to be more mindful of the officers than your peers. These people are not happy to be here, half of them are a step away from retirement and a third of them are trainees, others have worked in facilities and have had some type of disciplinary action against them so they were sent here to work. And work they do, as opposed to those who are in a non-reception facility where most officers just lay back and get a check. The officers here are going to talk very nasty to you with extremely foul commands out their mouth. Do not feed into it; be easy and hold your head until you get out of there and on to the next facility.

Once seated in the pen the thirty or so of you new arrivals will be un-cuffed (free at last) and told to listen up. You will be instructed to face the wall and take off all belts, watches, jewels and to empty all pockets then place your hands on the wall. Next the officers are going to walk around to each of you individually and tell you "Take one hand off the wall and remove one shoe." in the manner in which the officers tells you. Once both shoes are off you will receive a body search by hand then ordered to face the wall again. One slip or movement too slow will cause you to get jumped, believe me I know. In my very angry youth I turned around and purposely inadvertently elbowed one of these manic-depressives in the chest after he lingered around my grippers too long during a search. The five of them jumped on me while the fellows of what was suppose to be "us" stood silent and still.

After the search and a meal that lets you know for sure that "this is not the county jail" (just tasty, not kidding here the food is much better but you'll get used to this slop too) you will be sent to a table for further processing. An officer will take your information by asking a thousand questions and then tell you to strip down to your underwear. You will be given a towel, a small bar of soap and a pair of canvass sneakers to walk to the shower area in. In the shower area the officer there will tell you to throw your underwear in the garbage-can and give you a special soap to start applying on your body. The officer will explain that the soap is very strong stuff and you are to make sure not to let it get into your eyes. The soap is a medicated liquid used to kill bugs and lice. The officer will watch and make sure that you get a good amount on your head, under your armpits and all between your grippers. After the soap sets in for a few minutes you will be watched to make sure that you wash it all off. Everyone will know who the person is who did not listen to the officer. It will be the clown or two with a patch over their eye for the rest of your stay in reception.

A few steps back while you were enjoying that very welcomed meal a convict worker came in the bullpen and took down your clothing measurements. Be very clear about your sizes and do not argue with this person, if they suggest a larger size get it, they know how the last shipment of state clothes came in (either too small or too big). Your first state issued outfit will be waiting for you when you step out of the shower. Now on to the next stage which is the haircut. It's all coming off so don't worry about how good of a barber this person is just sit back and let it go down.

Hey, look how nice everybody looks back in the bullpen, everyone is clean and has a new hairstyle and everyone is ashy. It will amuse you how different you look at a person once they've been stripped of the material garments and ornaments that caused them to strut with pride. How equal you feel and how not so thuggish they appear. This is a lesson that almost everyone will miss…that from this point on you are all in this together.

STATE SHOP

It will be either the night that you arrive or the morning after there will be a visit to the state shop. This is where all of your state issued items are picked up. Even though the worker took your sizes down earlier make sure everything is correct before you leave the area. Check all of the items—the shirts, pants, the coat, underwear, T-shirts, sweatshirt, and boots. If there has to be a change made the woman behind the counter is going to give you lip when you ask for it but damn that, make sure it's corrected. These sizes follow you as everything else in reception does through just about your whole stay in the state system.

Note: It would be best if you get all of your clothing a little bigger as you are going to gain weight and add on size soon, real soon

.

MEDICAL EXAM

The works are given to you here from top to bottom. Eyes and ears checked, chest x-rayed, blood pressure and TB test taken, everything. If something is bothering you let the doctor or one of the nurses know and they will get right on it here as well as put the information in your records. You will get a brief dental exam and a mouth x-ray. Not much can be done here as far as dental work other than extreme emergencies because no one is in reception long enough to receive a total mouth job. The only test that you will not be given is the HIV test. You can wait until you get to your assigned facility for that and I suggest that you take one at least every six months if for no other reason than for your own knowledge of your status.

The nurses are again going to ask you if you are on any drugs or have you ever experimented with any drugs. No, the answer is always no. You will thank me later for this.

TESTING

Certainly not the SAT's yet and still it is very important. A very basic aptitude exam to find out what your "needs" may be while in the custody of the state. This little corny test along with the information that your assigned counselor collects is what is used to determine your classification status, whether you need to be placed in a very structured environment (maximum security) or one with more room to breathe (medium security). There are going to be at least one or two people in your class who will mark down any answer on the exam, maybe one who will not take it at all. These will be the people who you will see at your facility unable to get a work assignment because they will have to sit in the class for "slow readers" (Adult Basic Education) their first year in prison no matter what their educational level might be. If that test is not complete or says that you need help you will be placed in a spot where they will "help" you.

COUNSELORS

Please pay close attention here, because if there is anybody who can mess your life around any further while you are held captive, this is the person who can do it. The federal, state or city social worker that does not have a warped mentality towards convicted felons is as rare as a multi-platinum selling hip-hop artist that regularly gives back to his/her hood. These are some of the most evil people that you will come across, some more so than the officers. They will lie to you in your face and make decisions pertaining to you without consulting you or may just plain do nothing with your file which really is the worst. I have never and I mean never come in contact with one counselor who I would say is trustworthy, especially when it comes to handling our

personal business as they are assigned to do.

In order to save you a lot of pain start from now and find a strategy within you on how to

speak with and get the most out of difficult people. I find it best to be courteous,

frighteningly assertive and grateful. There are going to be hateful people wherever you

go, some will be able to hide while others will not, remember this is not a place where

you will have many wins if you try to use anger while making demands. No, that's going

to give them good reason to mess around with vital paperwork. If you feel that your

questions are not being answered write to the senior counselor or ask the convict who

works with them to assist you, go to the law library and search the Corrections Law or as

a last resort write to the state division that handles the particular issue (s) you need

assistance with. The administration hates that but so what. You'll get the help that you

need.

MESSHALL

Food which is supposed to be one of our great pleasures can be a disappointment,

especially when it is purposely tainted to alter the taste. Combine this with the reality of

your belly being in knots because of the tension in the air and a trip to the mess hall

becomes as fun as rescue efforts at ground zero…dangerous, depressing, and tiresome.

This is a favorite post of the asshole officers, rules are followed to the letter in here. You see to deny food to a hungry person excites the loins of an administration worker. A quick rundown of the rules can be caught by keeping your eyes open, watch the person about three people in front of you and those behind that person. By the time that you are next in line you will know what to do. The major rule state-wide is that you are responsible for eating utensils the minute that you step in the mess hall. Before you are allowed to leave the area you are to show the officer (s) those utensils and "drop-off" on a tray where they are taken to be washed. If either the officer does not see you "drop-off" or you fail to pick-up a spoon or fork on your way in guess what—yeah, another fondling of your grippers by way of a pat down search.

Once more we come back our golden rule which is to "be on point". As we know by now everything that has to do with anything requires for you to have a dull spell on some form of line. We get in line at the grocery store, the voting booth, to register for school, to be the next baby mamma or daddy and at the morgue. However the line in the mess hall is a little different. There's thick tension in the air and everybody knows that you are new to the facility. How you ask? Because you don't know where anything is and you're looking around all wide-eyed and nervous like an out of towner in midtown Manhattan. Toughen up some soldier, its game-time.

Not enforced much, rather more of an unspoken law unless you run into asshole-officer or you are in a disciplinary facility, is the rule of facing forward while in line. There was a time that if an officer had to explain to you more than once to turn around you were "helped" out of the mess hall where you "hurt yourself" just enough to help you understand this rule. Of course not knowing what or who is behind you leaves you vulnerable to attack and only adds stress to an already nerve racking situation. Recall my advice about having your neck out. To overcome this dilemma you can use the basic defensive stance of a boxer which is called 45ing your body. Place your shoulder closest to the wall up against the wall using the leg on this same side as your lead step; keep your face angled slightly toward the back giving you more of a view from your peripheral. This will allow you to see where you are going and keep an eye on where you've been; you can then enjoy the tasteful grub and get on with your day safely.

Note: Unless you land in a facility that doesn't regulate food portions you are always going to be unhappy with your servings, especially when it is one of your own who is controlling the spoon. If the administration wants to starve you then you just have to handle that, but when one of your own is at the helm of the abuse it is another story. We should never participate in causing each other misery but it will continuously happen where you are. You will be extremely angry but this is not the place to address the issue, remember the person serving the food lives with you, see them elsewhere and straighten things out.

MEDIUM or MAXIMUM

The stay in reception could last anywhere from two weeks to a year or more depending upon your special "needs", as well as the amount of bodies that the state has room for at the time and whether or not you'll be going to a medium or maximum security facility. I wish for no one to ever have to go to prison but if you must let's hope that your stay is brief. If this is the case you will be in a medium, if not you will be behind the wall in a max. The main determinant in where you are placed will be the amount of time that the court has ordered you to do. Anywhere from having to do eight years on up is max time, seven years and down is medium time. For classification they also use your previous institutional record, criminal history and how heinous your current crime is. The difference between maximum facilities as opposed to a medium facility is simple on the surface; the max is a building with cells for you to sleep in while the medium has dormitories.

It is said that behind the wall all the true lions and wolves roam. Their egos raised a notch as if others who have never been there are by some measure weaker. While it is true that it does take a special kind of nature to survive behind the wall, it is also true that a person could do ten years in their cell not making a sound cowering in fear. So just because someone has served time in a max it does not make them "animal thug", a lamb is going to be real wolf-like when it has to fight for its life and vice-versa.

Since the contents of the rules are basically the same when describing the two, with only a slight difference to how strictly they are followed, I'll continue to handle each subject independently of one another while bringing notice to what ways the two are alike.

LIVING AREA

Behind the wall the cell is your home. The bunk, the locker, the sink and the toilet all belong to you. This can be a place of serenity in a hostile environment or an added burden to the bullshit it is clearly up to you. Your jailers don't care one way or the other if you live or die so it is on you to stay healthy and you do this by keeping your immediate space clean.

Most maximum facilities are old and been up for at the least 60 years and made entirely of brick and steel; excellent for holding in grime, mildew, germs and bacteria. There is no way for you to live dirt free in here so you must clean up often. Try to always keep an extra can of cleanser or an extra soap ball or two, this way you don't have to reach far or ask police for anything when its time to get proper. My suggestion for getting proper would be at least every other day if not daily. Germs grow quickly in this closed damp area, what was not there yesterday could be on your ass tomorrow. Also keeping the cell clean and in order protects you from the weapon and/or contraband set-up. Knowing where everything is, an out of place or moved item is quickly noticed thus calling for a self imposed cell search. You never know who may want to get rid of you or want you around for a little longer visit. A trick of mine is to sprinkle baby powder on the floor as

I'm leaving out, very lightly so as not to alarm any uninvited guest, this way I can check for footprints before walking in, remaining "on point".

Mediums are dorm areas filled with anywhere from 30 to 80 people and are down right filthy. You get a lot of people with many different levels of what we call clean, lot of people from many different backgrounds and social status. Your job is to be aware of your self as well as that other set of individuals. Of course there are going to be adjustments made on your part, your tolerance level will have to go up a few notches but others will have to move to your beat as well, the survivor will be the one who allows diplomacy to run its course. The noise levels will be at times ridiculous and the filth unbearable, and there will be no getting used to people walking around while you sleep. By far the worst part is the unbuffered contact with the officers.

There is no safe zone in a medium everything is out in the open and the officer roams free. Anything that happens outside of the facility that affects this person's life in a negative way and the dorm is at this person's mercy. Being locked-up is already a dangerous enough situation, so in dealing with these 'yahoos' you need to know that your life can change in a second. Here is an example of such a second.

While standing in my assigned room, a six-man room mind you, preparing tuna sandwiches for my partner-in-struggle and me, we run out of mayo. Telling me that he has some in his room we start off to go get it. We step out of the room and take two steps down the hall when a dude from the room behind us gives a shout-out. As we turn our heads to return the greeting I hear a loud thumb. Turning to see if my partner has fell or something worse, I see the officer in his chest and then he starts screaming at him,

"What are you trying to do kill me, are you crazy?!! You assaulted me give me your I.D. card!"

I'm thinking this dude has got to be joking but knowing the hate for us I know all to well that he's very real. Now my partner is a young dude and this is his first time in prison, he's not very vocal and is clearly scared so not knowing what to say he says nothing. I told the officer in a not to appeasing tone that we apologize and did not see him coming. This devil pulled his emergency response pin and in rushed five more officers and they dragged my comrade to the box. They made an attempt to have outside criminal charges brought against him and though it didn't go down that way it was a terrifying experience for him. He was beat up twice by officers while in the box and came out looking like a refugee from the lack of food and stress. STAY ON POINT!

SHOWERS

The protocol for most maximum security prisons across the nation requires that you receive a shower every other day…yes kind of foul right? Well this is a form of punishment and rather light if you ask me. The only time that you will really feel the effects of this is when the whole prison is locked down for one reason or another; you would only hope then that it's not for a two week to a month stretch. One of the ways to keep your self clean and showered daily is to be in a work program that has showers on the site, like the mess hall or the facility medical clinic. Many facilities have shower-houses in the yard or the gym, and after working out you can do your wash thing there but be careful because that person (or someone similar in character) is still in the area. The medium facilities vary when it comes to the shower set-up because the facilities themselves are very different, only a few of the newer spots are built alike. Some may have open areas in the bathrooms but most have single person sectionals, small sections though. So small in fact that there is no way an adult sized person would be able to spin around carelessly without touching the walls. Of course this is something that you should never do, many have suffered the ill effects from instant rash because of the slightest brush-up against these germ dwelling fixtures. I have not been in a prison bathroom or shower area that does not remind me of the smelly subway restrooms of the late '70s early 80s. The stuffiness, the dim lighting and the stench…Yuk! The kind of place that you were scared to use but you ran in anyway to leave a little something in the bowl then ran out. The only difference now is that this is a place that you will have to get used to using because it is "yours".

You will soon notice that the same few people will always be in the showers at the same time. Does this mean that these are the only clean people in the jail? Yes. It is by no means a coincidence that after catching a whiff of very tart body odor from a person that you never recall seeing them with any cosmetics in hand heading for the showers. Plain and simple some people are just not going to get wet. Others will have a locker full of cosmetics, a cell full, all of the latest brands with the prettiest of packaging only to never use any of it. Do not ask me why because I- don't-know-why. They are playing "show & tell" when the game being played should be "wash & dry".

The clean people aren't the only ones who you will constantly run into at the showers. Remember the clown from the county jail; yep you got it this person is up here too. No matter what time of day, what day it is or whether or not this person is scheduled to have a shower (as in a max) this person is there. Lathering up for hours and greeting everyone who comes in, taking forever to cover their nakedness, you know just always in the spot with people like "Damn, be gone already!" You know what; you guessed it I'm sure? This is the homosexual person. That wasn't hard to tell right? It may catch you off guard if you're not looking for it which most of us are not. We are dealing with so many other issues during the incarceration that a person who is not obviously living "out" as gay is of no thought to us. Be well aware though that they have been thinking about you. There is no mistake about it this person has not only taken this time to watch your grippers but has also tried to give you ample enough time to watch theirs. Now in other states the forced gang rapes may still go on but in New York State those days have passed from what I've been around. I'm not saying that they don't exist and that there are no more "bootie bandits" running around I'm just stating that it is not as rampant, so these shower games are tools willing participants use to find each other. BE ON POINT, KEEP YOUR MOUTH SHUT (wash and leave, no conversations) and WATCH YOUR GRIPPERS.

Note: Maximum security prison shower time is limited but do make an attempt to wash thoroughly. Your hair, breath, armpits, genitals, behind and feet all have their own different scent. Try to tap each one real good with that soap, you'll like yourself better for it and the rest of us will too.

PHONES and TELEVISION

"Slot-time" does not exist up here but you would think otherwise by how some of our peers perform for these phones. Here too you will see the same people using them at the same times weekly if not every other night. You may even see a person or two on the phones daily which is absurd to me.

Making the mistakes that you made to get yourself in this situation won't be corrected without some serious soul searching. You must get into yourself, jump into this bid of time and learn what you need to learn. Chasing what is going on outside of prison walls is like a fiend chasing that first high…you won't catch it. In addition to it being a distraction from what's going on around you, the calls are expensive as hell thus draining dollars from any help that your people may have the ability to bless you with. We know that these calls are collect so if your people are not going to refuse your calls take responsibility and budget yourself. Yes for certain you will need the conversations as a distraction but keep it to a minimum; you want to have access to your people for emergencies. The phones are not toys but if you play on them you will play yourself then your people will play you by blocking your calls.

The television is handled with less importance up here. The main reason for this is the amount of time that the population has to watch it. The administration works you to death, or have you participating in programs so much of the day that you literally have to set time aside to watch television. By the time that you finish doing everything that you have to do (work, work-out, cook, write letters, shower) it is time for bed. Almost all of the maximums have equipped the cells with a cable for closed circuit televisions which are great if you are serving fifty years, brrr. The mediums on the other hand have the infamous dayrooms. The same rules apply as in the county jail, only there is much more to watch on T.V. because there's cable television upstate and the 100 or so channels encourage curiosity which at times will cause a problem. It is a bit calmer than the county because you may actually have an extra television in some dayrooms, and with people learning a thing or two from CNN, TLC, A & E and the Discovery Channel sensible decisions are made. Still, you keep your head up; it does pop-off (get violent) on the regular.

WORKING-OUT

There's no doubt about it you are going to see some of the most beautifully put together bodies in prison. Any casting agent's dream, perfect expressions for any artist's canvas and any photographer's aphrodisiac. If you do nothing else in prison you will work-out…at least once. Exercise relieves stress and is a social bond builder, is fun, and you will love how you look in the cloudy mirrors after six months or so of push-ups, squats and curls. With all of the great things and feelings of accomplishments that are going to come from working-out there are also a few things to be aware of that could be not so healthy.

Having to go out to the yard for your work-out is an absolute fact and there's no way of you getting around this. This of course puts you dead smack in the mix of the sex and violence and hustling and police brutality that the yard has to offer. No matter how efficient you and your work-out crew are there are just some unavoidable hazards that will fall upon you. A stabbing may occur just five minutes after you all get out there ending whatever routine you were powering up for. There's also the officers' favorite game of not calling the recreation period on time causing you to lose these very essential minutes that is needed for the extra set. I have witness this create chaos among the more unstable convicted felons.

In knowing this you should always strive for the best results possible, keep in mind that you need to be realistic with your goals. There is no way that any of us are going to look like the women or men on the cover of FLEX magazine. This is not going to happen.

There are too many factors in our lifestyles that are different, most of which hinders our muscle growth. The stress, breaks in schedule and our diet are the basic obstacles, but having to work-out in the snow and/or excessive heat are muscle killers as well. All of this disturbs the recovery time that the body needs to heal in order to get big. Remember that getting some work in, with a balanced schedule is better than lying around playing with yourself all day, but more importantly the training helps you realize that your inner beauty will shine coming out of prison with knowledge of self and love for truth. Running to the yard everyday with the super hardcore attitude trying to look like Angela Bassett or some low budget Terry Crews in an attempt to get your significant other back in your life is not cool. It is also not cool to try to get big and lift everything in the yard thinking that you will be able to take over the jail. If you were a punk before hitting the iron you're just going to be a bigger punk after hitting the iron, no one is going to be scared of you. You should notice that the world's most powerful people physically look like a bag of cotton and pudding, and couldn't push thirty pounds off of their chest if their life depended on it. I am not being facetious here just look at Queen Elizabeth, Osama bin Laden, Vice President Cheney, Bush Sr., Gov. Pataki, and…well you get the picture. So don't kill yourself out there in the yard, the administration is trying to do that for you.

COOKING CREW

Many people fail to take the time out to really enjoy the art of cooking. Enjoy the use of flavors, the colors of fruit and vegetables and seasonings. The smell of each item used and the cutting and stirring and tasting. Cooking is a special kind of relaxation, that dance of the inner soul, one which you can share a part of yourself with anybody without the feeling of anxiety. In most maximum facility prisons you will find people who stay in their cells all day and just cook. They cook for themselves, cook for their people, may cook for you, cook for a fee. What they cook is nothing short of incredible considering what they have to use as cookware (small metal hot-pots, hot-plates). These people, my people, should be in four star restaurants somewhere for the way they'll make your tongue dance.

Listen here, I've had meals made out of 'crackhead-soups'…what!? Oh, now you don't know what 'crackhead-soups' are! You know those Top-Ramen noodles that your moms have all up in the kitchen cabinets that you probably sipping on right now…crackhead. Smile. Anyway, I've had people who dress those soups up like a Harlem girl dresses up a pair of $40.00 jeans. Oh you don't know about this either. The $200.00 belt and $350.00 sandals with a $110.00 t-shirt, accessories, the hips and plump butt and wha-laa…only a fashion fanatic would realize that the pants were from the bargain basket. She looks good and those soups tasted great.

Most mediums (not all) are cooking facilities that are equipped with stoves, microwaves, pots and pans. You know people are doing it well up here, right? Every medium facility that I served time in I had to have at least three separate cooking crews (from 2-4 people) because I work-out, so I must eat. You can not eat with just anybody though, a lot of people are very particular about who they eat with, the trick is to get along with everybody and you'll never have a problem. I had a Spanish crew, a Jamaican crew and a crew of adolescents for those late night meals (the youth are never on time). You can learn from your crew and teach them as well; this way we can breakdown all that racial bullshit that really has no substance, a racist is always a loser! However remember where you are at, never let anyone eat off of you without being a contributor to the crew. You can play 'Mr. Moneybags' big spender if you want to, people will surely eat up all of your food and leave you dry. Everyone has to play their part, one cooks and one washes dishes, and someone buys seasonings while the other buys fish. Keep it honest and you may find someone worth knowing.

VISITS

There is a great misconception about who is supposed to do this time with you. Read and understand this: NO ONE IS OBLIGATED TO DO THIS WITH YOU.

No one owes you, not a husband, or a girlfriend, not your "man you was getting money with", not your sister, your mother and certainly not your children. You did what you did to get there, you gave financial support to who you wanted to give it to, no one forced you to do so therefore it is wrong to try to force (by way of guilt or other means) someone to ride with you on this trip. Responsibility lies with us to make it through; it does not lie in the hands of someone on the outside, especially if they were not part of our lifestyle and have never been through this their selves. Those who have had a taste of this yet still don't come through for you to support are showing you moves reflective of how they are handling themselves out there, and if it is in a foul and/or felonious manner it is only a matter of time before they get another serving of this.

As I've said earlier you have to be very appreciative of anyone who may find the compassion and strength in their soul to stand along side you in pain and uncertainty. I often ask myself would I be able to do it, be able to come up weekly for a prescribed time allowed monitored visit with someone who I love. That may take much more patience than I have knowing how nifty I am with the pistol it would not take too many off those weekly sit-downs before…listen it would take a lot and we'll leave it at that.

The constant harassment, verbal intimidation and being treated as if they are the ones in prison adds fire to the feelings of disgust with the situation. Having to also endure the humiliation is soul draining; these people will make your 70yr old grandmother feel like an inner-city streetwalking crackwhore. Before she is allowed in the facility they'll demand that she shake her breast, take off her bra and/or raise her arms. They may even tell her to put a sweater on and keep it on and closed because her blouse is showing too much. Yes your grandmother. Now imagine the types of stares your well kept mother gets or the type of verbiage that is spat at your loving spouse.

I've learned that the biggest challenge for most of us is the toe to toe 10 rounder with our egos. Learn this and learn it quick…in there you don't come first. I don't care who promised you what, how many times you hear "I love you" or "I'll be up there this week". Know that as soon as that person sent off that letter or hung up that phone anything could have happened. They may have had every intention of making the trip whether being six hours away or across the street, things come up out in the free-society. You may have forgotten that since not a damn thing happens in there, but you need to remember real soon before you say or write words that will leave you without support. We do not come first, keep pushing to come first and when things get tight you will be first…first one to get cut off.

Note: Not feeling me on this huh, still mad huh? Well you shouldn't have been running around telling everyone that you were going on a visit this week. You shouldn't have had your behind all shiny, greased up and dressed in front of the television in the dayroom. On the day of your supposed visit stay calm and wait until you are called.

On the flip-side of this you should be semi-ready if you know that there is a possibility of you going on a visit, don't have your people waiting an hour for you to come out.

BUNKIES or ROOMIES

Living with another person can be a hassle. As individuals we all have a spirituality that needs space in order for it to be properly nurtured. As a progressive person matures we look for ways to fall into ourselves trying to find a place just for us. Understand how the first sign of adulthood is what…moving out of the family home right? Correct.

We know that as much as we love them even family can drive us up a wall. No one who knows me well would ever tell you anything less than remarkable about the love that I have for my mother and baby sister. There's no need to doubt whether or not I'd go back to prison because someone even thought about mistreating or harming either one of them. Those two are my soul and when I think about how much I love them sometimes I'm short of breath but would I live with them…hell no!! They are the sloppiest women in the world. Not dirty, just sloppy and there's a big difference. Sloppy is leaving magazines all over the table and shoes everywhere, finding lip-gloss in my leather jacket pocket. Dirty were some of our neighbors in the projects where I was raised with old chicken bones under the kitchen table, smeared butter with toast crumbs on their closet door knobs and jelly on the ceiling. How in the hell did they get jelly on the ceiling?! Nevertheless though you do get my point, we get tired of living with family at times so just imagine how it is going to be with a stranger for a Bunkie.

Whoever sat at the table of the think-tank that brought to reality this ingenious idea of crowding two or more convicts in one cell had to be masterminds or dunces. Sometimes the simple can come up with some effective stuff. Wife and husband can not get along all the time so you know two felonious strangers are sure to kill each other or at the least drive each other crazy. However being who we are we put the blows to this difficult arrangement. We learned to live with each other so much so that the new tactic is to change your Bunkie in the blink of an eye. If you have gone through this then you know the confusion, the drama and the anxiety that grips you. For those who have not let me explain.

There's an automatic shield that involuntarily goes up after we understand what pain is and what causes us pain, that shield goes up and we anticipate the hit, hoping that this hit is not the one that will get through causing us to feel that pain. Whenever a new Bunkie (a new stranger) is moved into the cell or room that you're in it is like a hit. The more hits you get the more anxiety builds, the more anxiety builds the more stress is manufactured in the body and mind, and we all know that too much stress is a killer. The administration knows that this system is very effective; either convicts are going to hate each other or they are going to get comfortable growing a like and concern for each other establishing a bond (which should be rare), in which case pulling one out of the area would disturb the safe-zone of the other. Perfect organized confusion.

We all should recognize that we grow and mature through learned experiences. Some walk through these experiences earlier than others due to cultural backgrounds, class status, or just by having more of an exposure to different environments. Where one person may have touched a certain time and space the other may not have. This does not mean that you are less of a woman or he is more of a man than the next person, however if a person has not had as many lessons learned as you or you as them it would be best to keep a safe distance. This will be physically impossible because of the smallness of the cell or room, which are always too tiny for one person so forget about two in a cell or four, six or even eight in a room. The distance created would be an emotional area, a mental area, allowing others (and you) the opportunity to reveal what they want to when they want to. Imposing yourself on others as well as giving ground for them to impose themselves on you could be a nasty encounter. We may never really know who the other person is or what the other person is capable of doing. One could be a cop and the other a murderer, one could be an aggressive snitch and the other a passive minister; however the cards fall for you play them like a pro. Play your hand smartly, be cool and have patience and walk light. Do not play with ignorance and closed minded prejudicial movements or attitudes because that type of player in prison is always going to lose.

THE END

Back home, to stay.

HIP-HOP, SHORTEYES, and OTHER STUFF

Most people who are new to this situation will often feel like this is the end of the world.

True, access to the greatness of society is blocked-off but the sun still shines and

eventually you will have an unfettered amount of time to feed on its wonder. Time and

space become major enemies to the psyche of many causing those who are not in tune

with themselves years of stress. Stress has kicked me in the butt many a day so I know

how unhealthy it can be. Besides eating away at your immune system (bringing on colds,

tummy-aches, and migraines), stress will send your mental into the ultimate matrix. This

is what brings about the thoughts of "my mother is dying" or "my child's father is

sleeping with my sister" and "that officer is trying to get me…"

Organizing the use of time and space in a productive manner conducive to your inner self

is the best way to combat stress. Sometimes working-out with weights, receiving mail or

that occasional visit is just not enough. An excellent reliever of stress is listening to

music, and of course the music of prison is the music of the lower-classes: Hip-Hop and

Hard-Rock. It is said that music calms the savage beast though our jailers assume

otherwise when it comes to Hip-Hop and Hard-Rock, so much so that certain artists

material are prohibited from many facilities. The administration knows that the lyrics and

rhythms of liberation, justice, life, death, hunger, love and struggle are enough to keep

alive that rebellious nature in each convicted felon. The top administrators also know that

these two types of musical genres are very similar and if listened to properly could be racial gap closers, especially since we are already empathetic towards one another having lived the same poorness.

As of right now we can receive our dose of relief from ordering cassettes via an outside vendor, though this may soon come to an end. The recording industry is in the process of phasing out the cassette format which would practically dead the population from getting any music in. This will bring much joy to the administration that have the common knowledge to know that the only other format of music is the CD. It will take some time before CDs and CD players are allowed in facilities so keep your cassettes in good condition, and never lend them out without getting one for one from the borrower. Even your most trusted buddy will leave the prison with your music, more so if the tape is a classic or the current hotness.

Another very effective reliever of stress and aggravation is good old fashion masturbation. Jerkin'-off, gettin'money, rubbin'-off, button pulling, goin'up, teasin' Tammy or whatever else you may call it there's no questioning the end result…pure bliss. After a session I usually went right to sleep. There are a few who are freaky to a degree that they can still use their fond memories of a time before prison to work with but the majority of us have to use pornographic material. The magazines price range anywhere from cheap to expensive and contain subject matter that travels the realm from lame to superb production of fantasy and kinks. Everyone has there own slang names for these magazines some of the commonly known are 'Short-eyes', 'models', 'PaperPussy', 'Fuckbook' or 'Broads' by men. Women who usually don't make as much as a fuss over them as the men do use them from time to time labeling these publications 'sex book', 'Boys', 'EasyDick' and 'Bubbles'.

As with everything else keep an eye on your "work". Don't lend it to someone way on the other side of the jail or allow anyone to hold on to it for more than a day or two. It is common practice when one gets some new material or is loaned something that is hot to "handle your business" as soon as time permits thus eliminating any delay in returning something borrowed or "trading-off" as is custom.

You will also find people who play musical instruments, people who draw and even a few who sculpt. Yes, some real arts and crafts going on by making greeting cards, portraits, picture frames, wallets…Man I saw one dude who could put together movable action figures for kids using soap and dental floss. There are many progressive ways to work-off stress, masturbation and music just happen to be the most common, however they are also the most monitored by the administration. The federal prison system went as far as it could go in the courts to keep a ban enforced that prevented convicts from receiving sexually explicit magazines or photos, while all state facilities censor any music allowed in. Remember your jailers are lackeys of the government and the government knows the importance of taking away culture from the rebel-soul because of the power and influence it has. It doesn't help any that they also know that some of the most powerful women and men in Washington have a net worth less than a P.Diddy video budget.

MAIL

At this stage of the bid many still hold receiving mail as being very relevant to how they see themselves and how they feel others may see them. Not getting a letter at mail-call is a terrible blow to ones' self-esteem every time it happens, but there is no true way to protect you from this. I don't care if you get mail everyday and have twenty people writing to you, that one day or two when your name is not called or the officer does not stop at your cell will have you feeling very low even if it is just for a few minutes. On the other hand when you do receive a letter or two (even if its hate mail) there's a glad sensation that runs through your chest. Times will come where the effects of a letter will last for a week causing you to read it over and over again, bringing a much needed smile to your face.

As the months pass by correspondence between you and people on the outside will become infrequent, almost non-existent. There are many reasons for this but it's not only because, "These people are playing with my mail!" That may be the cause of you missing a scribe here and there but as far as no mail at all coming your way that's not it.

 Of course instead of just looking through the pages and envelopes for prohibited material the women handling the mail will stop and read letters, laugh at pictures and purposely on accident throw letters away. What you need to know is that the prisons hire low income people from its surrounding community, and these women bring with them all that their lives consist of. Previously the bar-fly, a farmer's daughter or married to asshole-officer.

Please believe that your mail will be delayed if she has a bad night. The sort of night where asshole-officer ran upside her temple for bringing him a warm beer, get the picture?

Though to be fair I will say that the women are not alone in this, most facilities will only hire two or three of them for this job knowing that the prison's population has more than 1500 men. That's real smart right? So imagine the back-up of letters if one of the ladies has that "sort of" night and can't make it to work. The results are the same as always, us receiving the worse end. Keep in mind for your own good, that irrelevant to what the administration does a constant flow of mail would produce at least one letter, so if you are not getting anything it means your people are not writing you.

LAW LIBRARY

The law library is much different up here, as oppose to county jail where you are trying to prevent a trip to the "big-yard", here you are working to get out (or cut the amount of years that you have to do down a bit). There is no hanging out or idle chatter it is strictly business in this spot. The first thing that you will notice is the seemingly endless amount of time that you are allowed in here coming from the fact of how empty it is inside. Most people have accepted the amount of time that they have or are too stressed mentally for the draining ride on the 'Law-Book Local', where every stop has major delays and the probability of changing directions while in route. Of course neither character fits the description of you, you want to get back to society as quick as possible and will not rest until you have done everything within your power to do so, right?! Good, just remember that balance is essential. Do not bust a brainstem in an attempt to become F.Lee Bailey overnight.

Navigating one's way through the hundreds upon hundreds of books, briefs, decisions and articles is no simple task especially for a beginner. The skill of understanding and applying law is not one that you fall out of your mother having. It takes a lot of reading and a lot of practice to get to a point where you know what you are doing not to mention becoming good at it. My suggestion to anyone in your position and sincere about changing that position, is for them to attend and complete the legal research course available at their facility. If there is no such course available, organize with your peers to push the administration to establish this type of course.

The quality of help that you will receive is also much better. There are convicts who have years and years of experience in dealing with the courts having had briefs or letters both accepted and rejected, they are familiar with the do's and don'ts of legal etiquette, frivolous arguments and openings for closed doors. A few you will find are excellent when it comes to researching—having the ability to quote penal law as if they were reciting the ABC's, while others will be better at writing briefs. It is very rare that you will find someone who does both research and writing well. When you do find that special someone this is who you would want to learn from, be careful though, all that law reading will have scraped away some of the person's social manners. Many of them are untrusting of others, withdrawn, and a few are arrogant as hell so be very patient and judge wise.

ASSHOLE OFFICER

The days of being threatened by the "Nigger-Be-Cool"- stick are far off in the distance but they are not gone. Many old-timers who you may come in contact with will be able to give you in great detail how heavy-handed a racist can become when given the opportunity to express theirselves. Recall what was explained in the beginning of the book—POLICE DON'T LIKE YOU! Most of them hate their jobs and hate themselves as much or more. However you can not tell who "asshole-officer" is by how they appear nor by what they may say, you can only tell who they are by what they do. You will come across a few who are going to have the foulest attitude, racist who are going to say some of the most outlandish things and others who will go as far as daily harassment but these are not "asshole-officer".

"Asshole-officer" is the one who intentionally tries to make your life miserable. These are the officers who go by the book, petty bastards, who will stop at nothing hoping to catch you in the wrong of the smallest violation of the rules. Not only do these particular officers go by the book but they try to create their own version of the book. If they write you a disciplinary infraction (a ticket) it will be written in such a way as to assure you a loss of some type of privilege, if you happen to slide by without a loss look for this officer to be back at you until they get you. A good majority of the time their own co-workers keep a safe distance away from them knowing that even they are by no way exempt from the BS.

There was once an "asshole-officer" whom I happened to be blessed with the ordeal of living under the care of that put the 'A' in the title. This guy had a name that was known all across the state's prison system, and you would assume that he'd have an ego that would match in size to that popularity but it was obvious that his self-esteem was shot. It didn't take a head-doctor to see that inside he was less than pleased with himself once you were witness to how he went extra hard performing his duty.

A Spanish brother who was not handling his nose-business correctly, using and selling Heroin with too many people aware of it (himself and one other) became this officer's summer long obsession. "Asshole-officer" knew this brother was doing what he was doing and that the brother was enjoying it. This angered "asshole-officer" to the bone marrow. Why would what a convict does to himself, especially if it is destroying his own life with drugs be of any concern to "asshole-officer" you ask? You'd have to ask him but I wouldn't advise it.

Anyway, like most of us the brother knew that the heat was on. Since his living area was being searched three times a week and his body frequently pulled over whenever outside the housing unit during movement, he figured he'd better stay on top of his water game (drinking a couple of gallons of water all day and keeping a jug at his bedside at night to assure that he'd pass any surprise test of his urine). However after this brother continued to test negative for drugs in his system "asshole-officer" had had enough.

I can laugh about it now but as it was going down I was quite frightened. Already in the learned habit of sleeping with one eye open gripping my pillow tight, the slightest shift in energy has me up and in the ready, so when "asshole-officer" trailed by four of his pals burst into our room at 3:30am I just knew that it was either we kill or be killed trying. As it turned out this man told the rest of us to relax while they snatched up this brother out of the bed and threw him on the wall to pat frisk him (he's in a t-shirt and underpants mind you), handcuffed the man and took him in the bathroom. After they "gave him the Business" for a few minutes he came back to the room and said that they took his urine, threatened his life and snickered that they finally got him.

Now knowing what I know and being incarcerated for the number of years that I have these incidents shouldn't surprise me. When I thought about it after the fact this incident did. You see "asshole-officer's" regular shift was 7am-3pm, that means he would have had to have had this on his mind at home during dinner with his family. He then got out of his bed up from under the arms of a loving wife, while leaving his children extra early to come and mess with a convict. This is "asshole-officer", and if this person gets on your case you will have a miserable time.

Most of the people who you will come in contact with will tell you that these officers were born this way and the truth is that the majority are. However do not make the mistake of assuming that there are none who were created, the mistake of not believing that some one (or two) on the convict's end helped to create these psychos. Officers are informed from the start of their careers about the dangers of trusting a convict, informed by way of horror stories of those who have lost their job (which many knowing that they can do nothing else see this as a career) because they got to dealing too closely with a "no good convict" who couldn't hold up, or was out to get the officer all the while.

Note: The only effective way for you to safeguard yourself from the nonsense would be to treat every officer as you would "asshole-officer" and that would be to stay clear of them.

PROGRAMS

To rehabilitate is to restore to useful life through education and therapy, or to reinstate the good name of. Unfortunately and impossibly this can not happen by sending one to prison. The essence of the environment itself is inconsistent with the balance of space and time needed for proper learning or healing. And you will find out that once you go through prison doors, the value of your name is worthless to most of those who think that they may never cross the line.

Parts of the so-called rehabilitation process are institutional (prison) programs. A few of these programs were adopted from outside of the penal system, Narcotics Anonymous (N.A.) and Alcoholics Anonymous (A.A.) are two of the most known, but many were created inside. Of the programs birthed from within prison walls, convicts from all types of backgrounds played the bedfellows that brought them to life, which at one time (because of the recidivism rate) caused many in the public to cry "FOUL!" They are claiming that convicts were not professionals' therefore inept criminologist without any true motivation for encouraging change.

The last thing that anyone who is behind bars wants to do is sit around an audience and discuss what vices (may or may not have) played a part in leading them to the pokey. It is very embarrassing, especially for some who are emotionally unstable, and it is very boring. As if being in prison is not boring enough.

Are these programs necessary? Well yes and no. Yes because of the fact that participation and completion of one or more of these programs is mandatory before an individual is even considered for early release. Necessary because refusing to program is the same as refusal of a work assignment which could get you some time in the box (about 90 days) to think your position over. Also necessary when applying for a transfer to another facility, however the programs are not needed if you are intent on serving out your full sentence, someone who has their thing together or knowing yourself—you've come to the point of not wanting to change the quality of your life because up until this day (even in prison) things is just peachy.

From my experience, and in my opinion, learning about something that one has no knowledge of or knows very little about is always a plus. I knew absolutely nothing about "recovery", having never dealt with narcotics or any other substance to get high, I literally laughed in the face of one of my assigned counselors when she said that I needed to be in a residential "recovery environment" to understand how others' addiction may have attributed to my life of crime. It seemed very funny at first thought and I didn't immediately take to the suggestion, but after a while knowing that there wasn't anything to lose I went on in. Now up until that point I figured that my contacts with addicts were minimal. Other than seeing them on the street getting high, being chased by cops or dealers, or even being on the same cell bloc (where I never spoke at length)—my ignorance of the effect that drugs had on our society and our individual behaviors because of it was in whole bloom. After sitting in session after session of hearing story after story, living with and interacting among the "residents", I realized that the "them" was a "we", and what separated us were the roles that were played in reaction to the disease. The program helped change my perspective on how to handle what was society when I was out there, what society is now, and where society may be when I am released. Definitely not time wasted.

Note: As with everything else in this country money is the underlining factor as to why these programs are made mandatory. The federal government tells the state government that out of tax payers' monies you are allotted this much to spend on crime & punishment. The state tells the facility administration how much they can receive for each convict who participates in one of the many programs. Then from the top down all those involved get some type of kickbacks (political swindle) off of that money, and each one of them is trying to keep a bigger cut of their own. The only way that anyone can benefit from any of this solely rests with you. Do what you have to do to get home; playing with these people and/or their money will just close another door.

WORK ASSIGNMENTS (JOBS)

No surprises here, same as in the street white people get the better paying jobs. It does not matter if it is an apprenticeship in a vocational trade or working directly with the administration; minorities are almost always pointed towards the less prestigious gigs. For the most part trust is the major determining factor when decisions are made as to who works around whom. Many of the civilians who work in and around prisons are white, and even though we all are convicted felons (regardless of race) they still feel more comfortable with someone of "their own kind". Because these people look like them they are allowed to handle certain tools, read and distribute certain paperwork, and even travel around certain areas of the prison. Amazingly though, since the 1960s ninety-two percent of all escapes (both successful and unsuccessful) were carried out by whites.

We can learn the character of a convict from the type of job that they have, of which there are only two types, either they work for their peers or they work for the administration. Working for peers would be a job where the population benefits from the labor such as housing unit porter, mess hall worker or a teacher's aide. Jobs in favor of the administration are painters, administrative runners (messenger), lawns and grounds worker and any type of clerk. As soon as you get a work assignment the whole prison is going to be watching to see how you perform, especially when it is in an area that directly affects the convicts. Everyone wants to know how you will treat "us" since there have been so many who have sold the convicts out for BS privileges like a little extra food, a current newspaper or just being able to converse with the civilian or officer that they work for. These are convicts who after holding these jobs for a while from the neck up start looking like officers and take on a whole new aura. I urge you to stay away from these types. Don't make them your enemies...no ever that, these are just characters that we never befriend and should be placed in the "passing acquaintance" bunch. Be slick with it though because there will come a time when you will be able to use one or more of these people. Nevertheless, be careful and remember that the people you are using will do anything to show the administration who's who.

FAMILY REUNION PROGRAM (Trailers)

New York, California and Illinois are the only states in the entire country that allow the privilege of trailer visits. These are visits where you, your spouse and/or immediate family are given 24-48hrs alone in a small house or trailer on the facility grounds. The federal prison system has no such program. I repeat the federal prison system has no such program…so yeah in the feds watch your grippers extra close.

Not all state facilities have the Family Reunion Program; generally it is a program for people who are doing a lot of time, therefore only maximum security spots were known to participate. Yet there are as of today four medium classification facilities in NYS with a regular rotation of sending out eligible convicts. Who is eligible? Basically anyone, but you must have a spotless disciplinary record for at least the previous year before applying. You know no major drug infractions or fights, and certainly no weapons or violence against staff charges. In the same category as regular visits, packages, the television and the phones, trailers are a privilege thus any major (and sometimes minor) BS will be used to nix your participation in the program.

The rotation for those who participate is one FRP visit every 90 days. This also varies according to the facility that you are in. A few of the maximum security locations are 8 hours or more from the city, and even though there is a substantial amount of time between one visit and the next there are a lot of people who will not make it every visit. Of course this will shorten the list of eligible participants and as a result you may end up in a facility where the rotation could be anywhere from 35-45 days. Not bad, but who in the hell wants to be serving 20yrs to life eight hours away from family for a trailer visit…understand where I just went? If you stay out of trouble you won't have to ever worry about this nonsense.

As stressful and overwhelming as serving time can be for all those involved the intent of the program is to help maintain family ties. This is not a letter, not a phone call or a regular visit. These are unsupervised hours of time that should be used for healing and understanding, time used to help one another get through this situation and any others so do not waste it. Just think how silly it would be to spend this time carrying on about that package you did not receive or that person that you caught your significant other hugging ten years ago. And please by all means, if you know that you are a couple or a family who can not be together without loud arguments and light pushing or shoving causing a scene, stay away from the program. Because if the CO's on duty have to intervene the family will be escorted off of the facility grounds and you will be taken to the box. Of course after that you will be disqualified from the program for the duration of your disciplinary penalization and a year or more after the time that it ends.

Okay, let's get down to the gravy and grits. You do the crime, you do the time. That time is a punishment, and the greatest punishment any human will ever go through is isolation. The second greatest is separation from the opposite sex. A slow death, any shrink or zoologist would agree. The Family Reunion Program has been a blessing, for any female convict who has had her "earth watered" or any male that has gotten his "nuts out of the sand" will bear witness to this. Just to be hugged, caressed or whispered to is enough to get you by a few months of BS. However we must not rush and run into a brick wall. Being locked-up is terrible but it does shield you from a lot of horrible stuff. Stuff like STD's, HIV and AIDS. Don't get me wrong, I'm not telling you that you can not get these diseases in prison; unprotected sex anywhere is down right dumb. But the majority of you are not going to get any loving inside so chances of contracting "cooties" are slim, so why after surviving this brutality would you cause your demise by humping a dirty penis (girls) or slapping meat to a sick vagina (guys).

The D.O.C. has taken the liberty to make a rule requiring that you send out a form giving the department permission to send out the latest results of your HIV test to your spouse and/or family before you are cleared to go out for a FRP visit. This protects the administration from any legal actions for any slip-ups; however it is up to you to protect yourself. Have your partner send you a copy of their latest test results. Being in love doesn't mean that you care for yourself less, you have to be thought of first when your health is at risk; there are a whole lot of wacky activities that people outside of prison walls are into and your people are not exempt from being placed in one of those categories. There is always a possibility for anyone to fall weak to their own sexual needs and if you left them out there freaky and they're willing to come into a prison to be freaky they may have freaked someone else in-between time. So in explaining this I am asking you to use the condoms that are provided for you as well as the protection that you are going to tell your spouse to bring.

YOUR MENTAL STATE

Suppose everything that you believe in was somehow proven untrue. Now suppose everyone that you care for started to slowly disappear and suppose what you thought were your strong points can in no way improve the quality of the conditions in which you are living. These are the basic elements of being in prison. Now there are people who go through these same symptoms in the outside society, however we are not dealing with those individuals, in this book we are speaking about us.

The inner-self can only deal with so much at a time before it begins to affect your manner of thinking. The back and forth ups and downs and constant clutter of emotions are caused by the uncertainty of your next move, as well as an unsafe space. The space that is needed for one to go inside of the self fearlessly to handle its demons and recognize the errors of its being, and correct those questionable areas in an attempt to lick its wounds and heal. The results of that unbalance are people who will need a lot of help, professional help, just to be functionally normal. Hold on now; don't mistake my use of the word professional to only mean a shrink…you know a head-doctor. There are many different types of professionals; you have ministers, teachers, and grandmothers. Just about anyone who can assist us in bringing our brains up to speed so we are not looked at as threatening or crazy when we come in contact with those who have not been exposed to the prison environment.

You will have quite a few extremely dangerous minds behind these prison walls but you also have a good number of brilliant and perceptive minds in the mix. Your survival will be based on how even you are able to balance the scale between the two. How do you do this? How do you create a comfortable zone, one that will allow you to block out the hysteria without being blind to it?

The answer will be different for each person, for each person must find their own way. I can only tell you what I did for balance, which may or may not help you in your search. You should keep in mind that I am no licensed professional, not in the sense that the outside population would expect, so don't come looking for me if my ritual does nothing for you. I may not have a degree in psycho-therapy but I am the top graduate of the school of giving "A GOOD SWIFT KICK IN THE BUTT".

After a good night's rest or after every powernap, from that very moment that you realize that you are awake—don't do anything! Keep your eyes closed and take a deep, deep breath. Then smile to yourself and say aloud, "I thank the universal truth and the absolute laws of nature—for protecting me, guiding me, and giving me the strength to endure the imperfect. I will attack with vigor making progressive moves."

The key here is to make this your first thought and have these as your first words. It took a while before this became routine for me. I would slip-up a lot and either open my eyes first or forget to take that breath. To help me soak it in I would say my little appreciative phrase anytime during the day or night when I felt drained. I sort of willed it to provide me with an aura of divine energy that became a shield bouncing off tons of BS. You will see that in prison people will work on specific parts of their being whether it be physical, spiritual and in a retarded way emotional. Nevertheless they leave the mental alone as if it has everything in order, as if it's the best part of the fruit…a disastrous error.

We all have the potential to be (if not already) very dangerous people. A danger not only to others as those who are fascinated with the idea may enjoy, but also a danger to us. To be successful and survive inside as well as outside of prison walls there must be a growth in the development of compassionate reasoning. Not so much as to fan out the flames that are needed to sustain the harshness of our environment, but rather for the purpose of keeping sensible hands controlling the fire.

FRIENDSHIP

Most people who have done time or are doing time in prison will tell you that you have no friends in prison. I am not one of those people. True friendship in prison is rare but not impossible. I do not suggest that you search for this friend, confusing my earlier statement of being "ON POINT" with what I am going to explain now. Always remember that balance is what you are striving for and when it comes to friendship in prison you will at some point have to allow someone in your personal square to some extent, while also knowing who and when to keep or kick someone out.

Knowing the difference between a friend and an acquaintance is of the utmost importance. Prison is the breeding bed of emotional leeches, individuals who can and will sap your whole essence with just an hour conversation, exchanging your divine energy for their stress. It has happened to me all too many times, not fully opening the door but giving it a little crack and in comes "Mr. Dump-my Shitonyou". I learned hard and fast that these as well as other characters should be kept at a distance, a safe distance. You see unlike the outside where adversity may not show its face for many years, in prison the principle of togetherness comes into play as it is tested daily.

There is no one true gauge that can be used to determine how healthy a person is to be around. A major mistake that people make is thinking that because a person exchanges pleasantries with them, because that person talks sports or Hollywood with them that that person likes them, when in all reality that person could give less than a damn about them. Never let it leave your mind that you are coming from a life where you received love or at least people feigned some type of care for you to a situation in which you will not get squat, if anything pure hate. We all become vulnerable to that person who may have the same interest, know some of the same people or drink the same brand of coffee; especially after the trauma that came with being abandoned by family, friends, etc. However with a little patience and learning of self we can avoid becoming victims twice over.

I have a friend, a very good friend. My friend knows and understands who he is and knows who I am. My friend would not place himself in a situation that has the slightest possibility of developing into something crazy because he knows that whatever he gets I get. He has the same concern for my family as I do; he calls and writes my family as I do his. I argue with my friend more than a little bit because we don't agree on everything. He gets angry whenever I wanted to resort to an extortive handling of those around us, and I step to him when needed. I feel good when I see him and feel even better when good things happen for him. We deal with each other as men having respect for, as well as a responsibility to ourselves.

An acquaintance is that person who may have the same work program as you do so you make sure to give them the newspaper after you have finished reading it. You may meet up with them at the same time during the week to play chess or trade music. You may even share a meal or two with them. Will you feel good when you see this person, can they make you smile and forget the rough morning that you were having? Yes of course. Do they have open access to your food locker, get to see photos of your brother or have your home address at hand? Hell no! The sooner that one learns the difference of the two the safer one will be. Everyone that smiles at you or gives you a cupcake does not have your best interest in mind. One should never be a dummy of ones' own ego.

RELATIONSHIPS

The mode in which a person or thing is connected with another; connection by blood, family, kinship or marriage. These words are the general way in which we define relationship. It is one of the hardest situations to be in, a letting go of self at times, and an exaggeration of selfishness at others. Whether it is woman to man, father to son or teacher to student in this day and time the strains of keeping a healthy relationship intact are enough to cause ulcers. Add to that pressure the reality that one of those persons involved is in prison and what should be a joyous human point of existence transforms into an almost impossible task.

Any relationship worth having is never hassle free, and boy oh boy there is no more of a hassle than dealing with someone in prison. There's a difficulty with communication because of the gap in time and space needed for common understanding, and without communication no relationship will endure. In prison everything that you learned, read about or dreamed of on how to deal with each other as people will be challenged right along with how we deal with ourselves. Let no one tell you anything different, a commitment to someone in prison from someone on the outside is about as easy as winning the Powerball Lottery—two years in a row. However if someone makes this promise to you do your best to make them walk in those shoes.

To stay in step with self when dealing with any relationship, a person can not feel that they are coming from a position of weakness. You have to know that because of where you are at your role in a partnership is no less meaningful than the other person. This will stop you from accepting what people are willing to offer as oppose to getting what you need. Any person who feels as if they are coming to save you will bring a distorted picture of themselves and the purpose of the relationship. That issue will carry over into how they treat you, always leaving room for a breach in any union. The same can be said for the person who may feel that you will be able to save them. Of course you will show an empathetic face, give advice and a hug or two but your true support for them would be a commitment of intangibles; dry promises and obstructed displays of meaningful solution. For either you or them to have a winning result at the close of this task all parties have to come to the table viewing the situation as raw as it is.

There will be people who will do what you feel is everything under the sun for you. Their's are the only letters that you will receive and only visits that you will enjoy. You are only able to call them on the phone, and it is no surprise whose name is on that package you just received. Be smart though, never settle for less and don't fool yourself into thinking that you are getting any more than you really are. Rarely will anyone overextend themselves for you, it happens but it won't be a regular practice. Believe me if they are doing it they are doing it because they are able. The visits every week no matter how far away you are, all the money orders, the boots and radios are what they are…nothing more, nothing less. All this could be looked at as very major to you but very minor to them. A lot of people have their act together out in society which makes doing for anyone in prison very recreational. Your job is to know who and what you are working with, if there is a genuine struggle for your people to ride this out with you don't blow it by being ignorant. On the other hand if you want to find out just how serious someone is take them out of their comfort-zone. Make it less easy for them to do for you.

Nine times out of ten at the first sign of distress these very supportive people will be looking for an out. It is essential for you to find out if those who proclaim to have your back are there for the long haul. You see this is only the beginning of the end of your rough trip.

PAROLE BOARD

Okay. It is time for you to see "the peoples". You have shown some major discipline and completed all required programming, learned a few trades and changed a few of your old ways. Whether it has been a third of, one half of, or that number in front of your life term you rode that time and broke it like a cowboy does a bronco. I'm proud of you and you should be very proud of yourself. Never let anyone play it down, this is as great as an achievement as graduating with a degree, birthing a child or selling a million records. You have survived, you were pushed and you pushed yourself. Good for you! Let's keep the celebration short though, knowing how the war is far from over.

Going before the parole board is scary, there is no other way to put it. Whether it is your initial appearance or you have been there ten times already, you know that whatever takes place in that room will determine when or if you are going to get out of prison (or so we've been hyped to believe). For two weeks prior to the actual day a little bit of every emotion will run dumb through your body, from anger and rage to extreme giddiness and grief. It's possible and likely that you will go a few days without any sleep then turn right around and sleep until the next week. Thoughts of how ready will you be and what will you say, or what are they going to ask you will stuff your brain. You know, all of the elements of straight up stress. However do not allow it to become an all consuming stress that stops you in you strut, let it fuel you knowing that whatever the outcome you are going to be fine.

In my experience the most overlooked bit of information given to anyone about to appear before the parole board is who is on the board. As with certain judges and district attorneys, a few names of board members are going to be heard of and known as hard-asses but no one seems to give up much more information on them other than that. As of this writing I don't know much about them either, but the little that I do know about the character of these people should help you build an idea on how to present yourself in front of them, as well as what your chances for release are.

You should first know that the governor appoints the board members to their positions, so a hard-ass governor equals a hard-ass parole commission. The governor is going to pick these people carefully, remember they will have the power to send you to the street; it's not in the best interest of the state to have a softy on the team. These are people who are firm in their beliefs, they are anti-crime and anti-you. They come from highly centered backgrounds such as the military, law enforcement, select branches of the judicial system and the most conservative of the political parties or social elites. My last parole board appearance was before a retired general (33 year veteran of the Army) and a former head of the state's probation department. Now imagine if I were to go in there with a half wrinkled pair of prison greens on and having caught this current case while still on parole. Exactly…I would be done off.

Could you prepare for or prevent the denial of parole, the backbreaking two year hit? Well no, not in the way of just knowing who is on the board. Even when you take the time to find out whom, you will never know which members will be there when you are scheduled to appear. In NYS there are 10-16 members, but what you can do is practice speaking.

Many of us feel that at anytime when asked we would be able to run off a million words about the "what's", "when's" and "why's" of the events that lead up to us having to sit across from these people. This is far from truth and rarely happens. The majority of us get so nervous that when we open our mouths the words won't come out. Sort of like that first time you put that gun in somebody's face or stood on that corner making that first drug sale. Remember how fast your heart was beating, how sweaty your body got, the way you almost messed your underpants up? Well that's the feeling, you were a punk then and for a minute you're going to be a punk all over again.

Practice makes perfect but there is no perfect parole interview. The questions move in many directions, come from all over the place, and they are asked in ways that are set to anger or confuse you and there are no right answers. So how and why do we practice? Well the reason for why we practice is simple, we have to learn our stick points, the things that may be done or said that could cause you to verbally stutter and/or mentally lock. It is important to keep a steady flow mentally and verbally, a confidence that comes from being sure of yourself and what you are saying. Similar to the way the courses on how to prepare for a job interview are given with repetitive oral exercises that gets one accustomed to relaxing nerves, you have to take time out for yourself to make sure that you get the best out of yourself for this chance at early release.

How do you do that, you ask? Well one way is to speak in front of a mirror. Write down possible questions that you may be asked at your parole hearing or ask an associate of yours who may have been to the board already to let you view the copy of their hearing minutes. Better yet ask them to write down the questions for you, this way you won't be swayed by knowing their responses. As you stand in front of the mirror look down at the questions as you are reading them, then look up into the mirror when you begin to answer them aloud. If you happen to be a shy person this will get you used to looking people in their eyes when talking to them. Another way for you to practice is to set-up mock parole boards. For some this may be difficult as they may not want anyone to know what they are in prison for. Nevertheless you must make the decision, either embarrass yourself in front of your peers or make a fool of yourself in front of the board. Good choice.

Of course you are going to do this with the few people that you trust. People, who will be honest with you, articulate, willing to help and have been there quite a few times already. Usually these are going to be the older more seasoned convicts around you. No games, everyone involved has to be serious keeping in mind what you are preparing for. Let them know that they should give it to you raw, and when it's all said and done you must respect their critique. Go back to your cell, room or cube and analyze what was said as well as how you are going to attack it the next time. The sooner you start to prepare for the board the happier you will be with your performance and in the end that is what's going to matter.

As to what the parole board wants is another trip entirely. The basic understanding is that they want you to show remorse for what you have done, take responsibility for the crime and admit guilt. Now you may still have a chip on your shoulder and may still be in denial about what took place but remember you are in front of those people for a reason, they have a record in their hands of a conviction with your name on it. Your ego is what may have helped get you to prison, don't allow your ego to keep you in prison. If you copped to a plea or were sent up on a jury's verdict it is silly to (though very often done) go in the parole hearing trying to dance around what they already believe to be fact. That will leave a lasting impression of you being deceptive, a slickster, and that's not good at all.

They also want you to be beatdown, a person with no fight left in them, totally defeated. They want to feel as though they know prison has broken you. If they look in your face and the look of a timorous person is not in your eyes you won't be back on the street anytime soon. The administration is aware of its system and is fully aware that there is no such thing as proper rehabilitation, so in essence there is no real incentive to release you. However with the hopes of smashing your spirit by denying your release and an added bonus of extra money for the state keeping you caged, your jailers feel like winners when the board says no. It is in the best interest of no one to let you go.

Now let's take a logical view of the situation. We have a violent child that was locked up at the age of 16 maybe 17. This child's character is formed behind prison walls for 10 years becoming an adult with no rehabilitation. Would you feel safe sending this person back to society? No. So you deny this person parole once, twice, three times. You deny parole until you can not deny parole anymore. Have you said that this person is unfit for society?

Well in black and white on paper, yes you have. What has in fact really been said is that no one can tell who is ready for society from a 4-5 minute interview. What is being said is, "I don't know you now and I didn't know you before the crime, but I do know what we have done to you as an institution of punishment for that time in between." This is what we are up against…this type of logic.

We here in New York State prisons have the extra burden of being the top money earner for the state. While other states have as of recent released large numbers of felony offenders because of over exhausted budgets, New York has no such problem. With New York being one of the poorer states agriculturally it is dependent upon the industries of the prisons, where other states are losing money with crowded prisons NYS is gaining. What has to be said is that there is no real plus when you send out bunches of angry, jobless and disenfranchised cons to the street. No one wins.

Note: Before you leave that seat in the parole hearing make sure that you have said everything that you want to say. Don't give up too much information; if they don't ask don't tell. Once you leave though there is no coming back so open your mouth during the interview. As always if you do not receive a favorable decision—appeal it.

PAROLE (DENIED)

Okay, so now you know that you're not getting out as soon as you had hoped. You are very upset and that's understandable, it is a major disappointment. I've been there as well (twice); my parole board hit was so heavy that it felt like I was trying to leg-squat with six hundred pounds on my back. This is no time to do anything that will take away from your growth. Fall back and get away from everything for a couple of days. Clear your head and prepare your appeal. All those ideas, plans and dreams are still possible; you have just been given time to make those plans a bit more precise and those dreams a little bigger.

PAROLE (GRANTED)

Well, well, well. You made parole and have a release date, congratulations. You did the damn thing. Be proud of yourself again. Absorb yourself in the moment, lay back and suck every drop of it in because it will be short lived. That's right it's not over yet so don't start giving away all of your stuff or telling officers (especially "asshole-officer") to F-Off! You need to be more on point now than at any other time during the bid.

In most states you will now have from two weeks to two months to tighten your act up. There is a lot that has to be taken care of, and even though you may still think that your day is not going to come you are wrong. So as of right now while you're all excited and bugging-out hear me! Do not tell any more people that you have a release date. I know all of your crew is aware of it as well as the prisons' nosiest that work in the law library. You can't prevent that from happening, this sort of information travels through the spot as fast as a warning of who's the new snitch. Just do your best to keep it under wraps, a lot of people will not make parole, some may never. Some of those who will never make parole are bitter and would love to destroy your shot at the streets. The release date that you have been given is not permanent, not guaranteed, one misbehavior report (ticket) is all it could take for the administration to have that date snatched from you.

This is the time for you to start as we say "falling back"; you know to be less seen. Remember out of site out of mind, the faster you disappear from the daily conversation of other convicts the safer you will be. Even that little work-out team and cooking crew will show different faces once you make the board, no one wants to be left behind. Give them a little room as well until they can deal with the fact of you getting out of there. You may want to change your work program, change the time that you go to the yard as this will help you get that restrictive pattern of doing things out of your system. Start to get all of your paperwork in order, especially anything dealing with the address that you are going to be paroled to. Have whoever it is that you're planning on living with call the Division of Parole office in that area to make sure everyone is on the same page as far as dates, names and times are concerned.

Most of the people who were released and came back, released again and came back again, then had one more time for good luck always said the same words when asked what happened, "It was hard out there." One of the reasons that we have such a difficult time with the jump from prison to the outside is the lack of preparation on our part. The prison programs that handle the tasks of and supply information for those on the way out of jail such as Pre-Release and Transitional Services are no where near helpful enough. Am I suggesting that you skip these offices? No, I would never do that. You will need all that is available to you and though limited there will be something useful in those offices, but most will be programs or information that will work once released, you need to plan from now.

There can be no one set plan of action for any of us. There are just too many variables of situations involved such as how much support we will receive from family, who will the parole officer be, will we really be able to secure jobs and the list goes on and on.

A good start for anyone who is serious about never returning to prison is to write your plans down. Many of us have a bunch of ideas in our heads but never know how many flaws these ideas may have. Writing these ideas down brings to focus what may have been overlooked. Study what you have written down, go back and forth over it honestly and concentrate on what you can do to improve the plan. Add in your plan a few extra "ifs"; ask a lot of "hows", fine tune your plan so that flexibility and persistence are constant factors.

Get the newspaper and begin going over the classified ads. Look for places where you may be able to get an early jump on by sending a resume from where you are. Search for trade schools, training programs and anything that can be used as an entrance back into society. Ask for help too. Family, friends, friends of friends, even contacts from the few acquaintances who may be right next to you; anyone who you are in touch with that is employed and may be able to assist you by securing an interview or maybe a position.

There is one last matter that should be handled before the big day arrives. Catch yourself at a quiet moment, zone-out, for right now I want you to focus intensely, pick-up your pen and pad because you are going to write your last letter. This is a special letter, special because this letter is written by, written for and sent to ...you. Well just what are you going to write yourself? You're going to write yourself a nice piece of hate-mail. However it's not the type of hate-mail that you would get from some tripped out extremist organization. No, this letter will contain hate that will keep you in love with you doing you, or whatever other way you want to phrase "staying out of prison".

The key here is to dig, dig way back, back to the beginning of your memory of this whole mess. You could start it from the point of arrest or from the first time that you smelled what piss and old bars of steel taste like. At the instant that your disgust for your situation was born right on up until now and everything in-between, write down (and be specific) what you hate about prison. There is nothing too small, if you hate the milk write that down. If you hated the cold showers, the daily counts or stupid acting people write it down. It can even be personal issues such as you hating the feeling that you were a failure in life, or that feeling of loneliness. Write down everything that you had issue with during your stay, try not to trivialize anything. The letter could be as short as a half of a page or three pages long, it doesn't even have to be constructed as a letter you could just write a list. Seal it, address it to yourself where you will be residing at and send it out. Now don't open the envelope as soon as you get there because that defeats the purpose. Have it placed somewhere that is always within reach, and when you feel yourself start moving off-beat or you feel as though that job can kiss your butt, open up that letter and read it. Keep reading it until your silly-behind gets back on track. This will save you from what would be years of grief, while reminding you just how much you owe yourself, yes owe yourself to do what it takes to stay out.

Note: The average amount of time that it takes for one to start feeling herself is about sixty days from release. This is when we get selective amnesia about where we were and want to play "slick the system" so this is when most should open their letter. The more time it takes for you to open that letter the better. What you are really striving to accomplish is to stay so focused that you will never have to open that letter…one day letting your grand children read it to you after a Friday night's dinner.

ONE FOOT IN, ONE FOOT OUT

Once you are released from the custody of the State Department of Correctional services you have 24hrs to report to your assigned parole officer. This day is given to make sure that everyone has enough time to reach their city or town for the initial interview with their parole officer (PO), even if you happen to be released from a facility seven or eight hours away. By now I'm sure that you've heard quite a few people say that you should spend this time with family, maybe a little party or even suggest that you "hit the club", basically enjoying your first day out as much as possible for fear that as soon as you see your PO she/he will put the "clamps down on you" (i.e. curfew). I would advise you to do the opposite and make that trip to your parole officer your first stop on your way to the new life, the high life. The fact that you made it your business to take care of business first shows your PO that you are very serious about doing what has to be done while on parole. She/he may surprise you by not giving you your stipulations (see below) until your next visit, which could be the next day or two weeks later depending upon the impression that you made.

When you have your first sit down with your parole officer she is going to tell you what your stipulations are, meaning what you have to do in order to keep from going back to prison. Everyone has a set of stipulations and they may be the same or different according to the nature of the crime. Almost everyone will have some type of curfew, violent felons will have to take anger management programs, and alcoholics will have to go to A.A. The majority of the stipulations are mandatory; the ones that are not your PO may give you a little room to dance around. However don't try to do the Electric Slide or the Running Man as your PO will tell you, "You have one foot out, one foot in, how you move is what will determine if you get violated or not." My jewel to you is one of simple mathematics—cut the extra man out. Both you and your parole officer knows what the state wants from you, the thing is the state is nowhere to be found, sort of like a silent business partner that comes to put BS in the mix every so often but puts no actual work in. The essential relationship will be you and your PO, so ask that person from the beginning what do they expect from you as a parolee? Have them make that clear to you and let them know that you will do your best to make their expectations manifest themselves in your actions. If both sides stay true to what is agreed upon the relationship will remain smooth and you will have one less problem to deal with on the road to getting your life back in order.

GET TO WORK

As you can see you are not going to be able to just run around like a nut when you're released. You have worked hard at doing your time and getting out safely now you are going to have to work even harder. The most difficult task will probably be finding a job. And no not because you have a felony, for certain jobs the demand for workers is so great that if you're the best at what you do and can bring up that company the employer will look pass that fact. The difficulty will come from the job market and what may be out there, not to mention what you will perceive as a quality gig. Having a delusional idea of your worth is not a good start. Remember you do have a felony and have been out of the work force for some amount of time. Your competition will be people with degrees from other fields of work who have consistent employment records, students and moonlighters all of which may have clean backgrounds and will be seen as far less of a gamble to employ than you. It may take a while to find something that you really want to do, until then fall into a job that will feed that need of keeping your PO off your butt.

You are going to witness many of your fellow parolees run to social services (welfare) and/or disability offices in an attempt to dodge work. Listen; unless you really need these services because you have children or you are not going to be able to perform at any type of job don't go this route. Ninety-nine percent of the PO's are alerted to those on their caseloads who are not working and these are the people who they bother, you know they have that 'idle time is the devil's playground' mentality.

Nevertheless all jobs are not healthy environments for convicted felons. For example take a look at construction work, since it is the favorite choice of ex-offenders, almost all construction sites are dangerous work areas. To deal with the dangerous element of the job most construction workers are known to drink heavy and dabble with narcotics, for a recovering substance abuser this could be a bit too much to handle. These work sites also pay in cash, keep guns on the premises and are frequently into some violent mix with work coalitions, little rumbles that always end with police investigations. Investigations which include police questioning and for parolees that equal police contact; an incident that could sum up to a violation if not handled correctly.

Note: Though your search for employment is a bit exhaustive because unlike the majority—you have to safeguard yourself against vague labor situations that are actually common in nature, with patience and the lessons learned from your "schooling" it can be a successful outing. Mc Donald's may want you to be computer literate and hold a communications degree by the time that you touch street, but from your growth you have learned to be flexible and prepared to take advantage of any employment opportunity thrown in your direction. Always remain aware of your potential to be greater.

STREETS ARE WATCHING

For a while it will seem as though everyone and their Uncle Charles will know that you were just released from prison…this is not cool, very contrary to common belief. The least amount of people with knowledge of your status the better it is for you. Of course with this being the age of the internet personal information of just about anyone's background is becoming less and less exclusive. This does not mean that you should participate needlessly with blowing your own cool. Those who are aware of your status already…fine, those who are not aware of it should never be. People will/would treat you how they perceive someone who just got out of prison should be handled. This behavior will be based solely on that person's understanding of what has been put out as to who you are, not based on fact or your individual character, an understanding that could create problems.

You know that as a person you are changing, activities that were once very important to you no longer grip your attention. There are goals that you are working on, a new direction that you are moving in and a bounce in your step that is unfamiliar to those around you. Those who knew of your past will only remember what they choose to; usually it's that side of you that caused you to be away for so long. That past attitude of yours, the previous lifestyle and your reputation are all that comes to mind the minute that they see you. The threat that you may impose to their status, the distraction that you may be to the amount of attention they get will have people act negatively towards you.

Some people will do this outright while most will do it unconsciously not understanding what they are asking for. It is your job to be able to think for all parties involved.

The way you handled disputes behind bars is much harsher than the way society on the outside handles them, especially in this new age of "yapping-off" (calling police). What you consider a reasonable amount of pressure to back someone up off of you is just enough to send half the community running to pick up the phone to call the authorities. It doesn't matter how pleasant you were, how helpful, how loveable or how much of a bastard, creep and all around criminal you were that image of you has been replaced by someone who is much worse—an ex-con. Until it is witnessed, the belief of you changing will be a joke to some and thought of as an advantage over you by others. Staying out of the heart of the streets and away from old circles of troubled peers is the best way to skip over a bunch of nonsense.

As I mentioned earlier this is not the days of old, the days when you could tussle with someone and police come to calm things down then leave. The days where the worst that would happen to you would be a three day trip through the system, the days before you were a convicted felon. Those days are gone and have been replaced with a time where three days has now for you become a three year violation. You have to BE ON POINT. Walk down the wrong street and get caught in a police sweep—violation. Someone calls the law on you—violation. Anything that you may do and any place where you may go or any person whom you may deal with has to be heavily scrutinized by you…unless of course you don't mind a return visit. "Asshole-officer" would just love to see you.

Note: No one has a monopoly on violence and/or handling things. At any moment a situation can shift energy and we could find ourselves becoming victims. The children that you left behind are now adults with brains and muscles, guns and battles under their belts. You have been gone a while…be easy!

RUNNING TO RELATIONSHIPS

As soon as you get home people will be waiting and every one of them pulling for your time. Continuous parades of persons that include your parents, siblings, relatives, and friends and of course your significant other (s). In some form or another you have a relationship with each of these individuals and each one of them will feel that they're more deserving of you than the next one. No one is going to tolerate feeling slighted, it won't matter how they did or didn't stand by you when you needed them most, that selective amnesia is some funny stuff when it kicks in so as the hot product in or around the home you will have to establish some order.

The only way that you will be able to remain focused is if there are no shortstops on your journey to a successful stint on parole. It is important for you to have them understand that your time is limited, that you have an obligation to yourself to meet the demands of this new restricted way of life. You will not be able to do the things that you used to do or the things that they may want you to, new or old. They must respect just as you do, the fact that there is a new player in your lives. It is also important for you to keep in mind that no one is worth going back to jail for…and I mean no one! So if Grandma wants to see you but she happens to be on her last leg and living cross country, Grandma will get a picture or two sent to her. Your daughter's graduation is in the evening after your curfew, tell her "Mommy loves you and is very proud of you…here's the camcorder, make sure your father takes the lenses cap off before you all go inside the school." Are you hearing me? Good. Your PO can give you permission to attend these events however when you are fresh "out the joint" it is best to give it at least six months before making these request. As time runs everyone will get their minutes eventually, don't rush feeding into their novelty of your freedom.

Dealing with significant others will be a walk that you will have to take on your own. I am not a relationship expert, no one is. All of the people who claim to be knowledgeable on the subject, writing books and holding seminars and stuff are the same people sitting home playing with theirselves at night…single as a damn dollar bill.

 All that I or anybody else can truthfully do is explain to you about them and theirs. As with everything else you have read use what is helpful to you. We all have different circumstances, many variations and results of the union between two people. There is no right way, only a progressive way, a working way, a way that works for that couple. The hardest part will be to find out where you are as a person, especially after doing all of that time. You will have to know if you are ready to meet the demands of a relationship so soon after coming out of the clutch of a demanding beast.

Now it is very possible for you to do five, ten, even fifteen years issue free, nothing has changed for you—you may still be in the same mindset and still hold the same strong level of emotional boom for a person who you were involved with romantically, remaining stuck at the point of when you were locked up. The problem is everything has changed for the person that you may still be head over heels for. On the outside of those prison walls they've gone on with their life, experienced new people and maybe growing into a new set of values. There is also the flip side. You may be the one who is changing, the one who has maybe picked up an interest in religion or buckled down on their schooling, moving in a direction that can only better the quality of your life...while the person who you are (or were) involved with has stalled out. They may have held the same dead-end job for ten years, socialized with the same people and going through the same family issues. Issues that were there before you were with the person, while you were with the person and are still present now.

What I came to realize was that prison because of the time and space that I was away had the ability to forge a separation between me and mine that could have had us growing in opposite paths. That truth is all that I needed when determining whether or not I was ready for a relationship upon my release. The person who is close enough to be your partner may need more love, compassion, patience and time than you have to give. You may also need more than they are able to give you. As with any other relationship all difficulties can be worked out, having triumphed over one of the most challenging periods of your life pacing through the bumps of being with another person could be easy. Only after a sincere study of everything and everyone who will be involved will you know if you can hang tight with or should stay loving only self for a minute.

Since I mentioned loving self, there is another point of concern that needs to be up front. Having had to adjust to being alone, having to both consciously and subconsciously shut down empathetic emotions for others because of being conditioned by the lifestyle of prison—we are not the ones voted most likely to succeed at love. The people who you are going home to understand that (or should); you need to understand that as well. That forced isolation allows us to too quickly say—so what, so be it...whenever the calling off of a relationship is suggested. For people who believe in the conventional monogamous union, something most ex-offenders find absurd and after a long sentence highly unlikely, this attitude that they are not used to dealing with is seen as not being normal. Not being able to handle your resolve, or their bruised ego little things are made into big BS that could stress you out. Love yourself first, okay.

Note: There is no "catch-up", lost time is lost time.

SEX

From being locked up and without for so long the first thing that you will notice is that everyone is beautiful. Everyone is sexy. Every girl has a nice plump behind and juicy breast, and every dude has a bulge in his pants and big full lips. All women and men who have done a bit of time go through this. There is not too much of that being picky stuff anymore, looking for that perfect somebody is as old school as hardrocks slap-boxing in the building lobby. When you first get out that shorty with the cross-eye, rolling hip and quarter inch ponytail is looking damn good, not to mention you've never before realized how much sexual energy there is between the two of you. You can't believe it, after being home a week you found someone you can vibe with, someone who is ready to give you the business—suggesting that the two of you slide off somewhere and "get right". No doubt about it, you are with that! There shouldn't be a problem, everything should be good, you know this person well enough, and you spoke to them a whole forty minutes…right?!

Listen up Hot-Butt, slow down. You just got out of prison; there is no reason for you to run into some trouble that you really don't want. You have not had any for this long surely you can wait until you check the person out.

What you know for sure is the fact that you have not been with anyone sexually. You were tested months before your release and you are disease free. However everyone else is humpin' or has been humpin' and will be humpin'. They don't need you and you do not need what they have. In the years that you have been away society has become pretty loose, ecstasy and Viagra use is in full effect, and all of a sudden bi-sexuality (in or out, on top of or at the bottom of the closet) is so chic. Sexually people are speeding, people of all backgrounds and social status so if you mess around you will hop your fast behind into someone real hot, hot like fire.

The STD's that are out there are the same ones that you've been warned about in the past, added to that is the number of people infected with HIV/AIDS on the rise daily. Do not be silly and think that becoming infected could not happen to you. Remember how you thought that you were never going to sit in jail. Ask whoever you plan on "getting right" with when was the last time they were tested and ask to see the results. If you can not do this at this point in your life then you shouldn't be having sex. And if the person can not produce this proof of their good health then you really shouldn't be having sex with them.

HIV/AIDS are killers make no mistake about it, the 'clap' burns and 'crabs' itch. I'm sure that nowhere in your plans to get your life back in order have you made room for contracting any of this. There was time set aside for job searches, weekends with the children and maybe a hobby or two; but contracting an infectious disease in your love muscle that could be the death of you was not on the list. Love yourself; you deserve all the great things that your new life is going to touch you with. Protect yourself please; don't just have safe sex have the safest sex.

VIOLATE YOU DID

 The worst thing that can happen to you while you are working to get your life in order would be a violation of parole. Of course this stops everything. More than likely you will lose that job, your family will be heartbroken and those are the least of your troubles. Man, you are going to wish that that was all. A violation of parole means that you will be returning to jail (even if it ends up being only to fight the violation).

A bail is out of the question, so don't even think about it. Once the court is informed that you are on parole there is an automatic hold put on you, and if your PO is violating you herself you'll be taken straight to county jail. Don't start buggin' out, cussing and crying and stuff, which is not what's needed now. Your head has to be focused going into this next phase of "my life as a felon"—and pick your damn head up…don't start that feeling sorry for yourself garbage because you may not be the blame for this. I told you that this is going to be a long trip; we may have to stop more than once before we get there but we will get there. Now blow your nose and wipe your eye.

At some point your PO is going to serve you with papers stating the charges and what he/she is violating you for, also the date of your preliminary hearing. The PO is going to ask you if you are going to be present at this hearing or if you are going to waive your rights to this hearing (skip this and other preliminary hearings until your final hearing). I don't have to tell you that anytime someone asks you to give up any rights it is not good. Make sure that you state that you are going to your preliminary hearing and make sure that you sign that off on the paperwork. When you get to the hearing there will be a parole specialist there representing for you, a parole judge doing what judges do, and an administrative parole supervisor acting for the state.

Similar to how it is handled in state court both sides present their cases in front of the judge. You can have witnesses testify on your behalf, as the Division of Parole will call their witnesses who are usually the police and/or your PO. After the evidence is heard both sides haggle over how much time or if any should be done. Rarely does anybody walk out of parole hearings without getting some amount of time to serve. It does happen in cases where there is no violation of parole and it is obvious, but it is very rare. The amount of time agreed upon by both sides (or if no agreement has been reached) will be presented to the judge at the final hearing. The judge can roll with either of the parties or make her own call which you would think is it, but it's not. When all that is finished the judge sends everything to the division at the state level knowing that they are the ones that will make the decision in the end.

The usual amounts of time given for a violation are any one of these:

a) 90 days   b) 6 months   c) 1yr   d) 18 months   e) 2yrs

The violation that you would receive is based on how many of your stipulations were broke and whether or not this is your first violation. First time violators usually receive a) or b) repeat violators should look to walk out with c, d, or e. In receiving your violation know that you will be doing everyday of it, there is no early release from a violation. What you get is exactly how much you will do; you can set a watch by it and your people know when to expect you back home, your boss could be given a date and asked to hold that job for you. However once again there are a select few who will not have such a clear path from one point to the next. You guessed it—us, the violent felony offenders, how'd you know?

In New York the Division of Parole has saw fit to separate the men from the boys. Instead of everyone falling into the same guidelines when it comes to violations of parole they have now instituted categories. Numbered one, two and three, each one of these categories alerts the state to which amount of time you should be given. Numbers two and three categories are for non-violent felony offenders and could receive either a, b or c. Category one is for the violent felony offenders and those who fall in this category could receive d, e, or more. Yes that's right more.

Let's say that you just finished a five to fifteen year bid but out of that sentence you end up doing seven years because you were hit at the parole board once (violent offenders almost never make their first board remember). You get home and you're doing well. You have a decent job, the kids are in love with you and happy again, and you have a new lover not to mention that every so often you give your ex a little taste. Hey, you are killing them out there and for four years there's no stopping you. Then it happens, boom, you get popped. You missed a visit to your PO and when he calls to find out why…you were not home thus breaking your curfew. Damn, two charges, not a lot and besides your PO is cool. Well today just happens to be the day that your PO was barked on by his supervisor because someone else on his caseload (who was on the run) just made the news with a robbery-homicide. Yeah your butt is toast, there is no getting around that, so let's go find out just how long your stay could be.

The time that you served in prison combined with the time you were serving on the street (dig the language people) leaves you with four years that you owe (on paper) to the state. The initial request from the state will be for an 18 month violation. Sounds like a long time for a couple of minor mistakes and it is, but this is how they are giving it up now. The drama comes though once the state receives your papers because they can act a fool if you don't accept the first offer and opts to challenge the violation. As category 1 the state can get all the time that is owed by you. Which would you rather you do, the 18 months or the 48 months? That's an easy answer right? You'd be surprised at how many people still after all of the lessons learned play games with the system as if it is not dead serious about taking you out of society.

Knowing how hard it was just to get out of prison and knowing that if they could the state would have never let any of us go, we have to guess that a person is a little off when that person thinks that an honest process takes place to determine your freedom—especially after you've been convicted of at least one felony. All fairness is out the window, but in saying that I would never advise anyone not to put up a strong fight to avoid prison. I only want you to know when to take those light blows and slip the heavy ones.

LISTEN UP

Whatever your hustle may be, selling narcotics or selling sex, picking pockets, robbery or investment fraud it is only worth it until you get caught. Then all the fun you had, all the power and all the money will be what it was, all for nothing. Serving time is becoming harder and harder as the prison industrial complex is moving, growing and stuffing itself with attitudes of the past. Prison in all its darkness and fright forces one to dig deep inside of the self searching for new methods of survival, as human beings we have to learn a new level of patience and an extra tolerance of the abnormal, but never an acceptance of your existence there. You will never adapt to the conditions, only animals are able to do that because they are not aware of 'tomorrow', 'now', 'what I did' or 'coming from'...we are not animals. What we do is make adjustments, transform, and create a space that hopefully will sustain life.

Doing hard time will cause one to become too good of a student at making these adjustments. This will send you back out to society in a strange manner, one that could help even your closest loved ones to leave you the hell alone. My people were tired of my stuff after a while. Cutting food with aluminum can tops, taking showers with underwear on and telling moms that I get on the phone at 8 o'clock…tired of my stuff, getting into bed with my boots on, telling the kids to lock-in for the count…tired of my stuff with the taking of bread from the dinner table to the bedroom and stashing it for later, and the running next door and scaring the neighbors trying to trade CD's 'after chow'. They were tired of my stuff and kicked my crazy-butt out. Don't have someone become tired of your stuff.

Note: With all the different challenges, relationships, people and dilemmas that you will face always remember when all else fails for you in an attempt to get your point across to a less than understanding individual don't wild-out. Just picture that person in state-greens or county-blues, imagine how they would perform and then treat them and the situation accordingly.

10 KEY Don'ts

1. Don't mind other people's business

2. Don't trust administration

3. Don't deal with homosexuals (unless of course you are homosexual)

4. Don't sit or stand with your neck out

5. Don't gamble

6. Don't worry about the outside world

7. Don't sell or use drugs

8. Don't travel heavy (with many bags)

9. Don't get involved in business that is not yours

10. Don't deal with anyone who does one or more of the don'ts

BOOK LIST

In order to correct our errors the study of our moves is a must. The awareness…of our potential to be greater, and to stand as political individuals with a purpose can only come from what we intake from life experience, and reading. These books (read in the order of appearance) provide clarity for the reader on her/his path towards self improvement.

ASSATA	Assata Shakur
To Die for the People	Huey P.Newton
Part of my Soul went with Him	Winnie Mandela
Black Power	Stokely Carmichael
Shoot the Women First	Eileen MacDonald
Soledad Brother	George L, Jackson
Woman, Race & Class	Angela Y. Davis
This Side of Glory	David Hilliard
The Black Woman	Toni Cade
The Wretched of the Earth	Frantz Fanon
Stolen Lives	Malika Oufkir
The Physics of Angels	Matthew Fox & Rupert Sheldrake
The White Boned Demon	Ross Perrill
Blood in my Eye	George L. Jackson
Pedagogy of the Oppressed	Paulo Freire

War in the Shadows   Robert P.Asprey

The Hero with an African Face   Clyde Ford

All God's Children   Fox Butterfield

Visions for Blackmen   Na'im Akbar

Stolen Legacy   George G.M. James

City of Quartz   Mike Davis

The Last Hardrock   Bliz